The Technique of
CROCHET

Pauline Turner

The Technique of
CROCHET

B.T. BATSFORD LTD · LONDON

ISBN 0 7134 51203 (hardback)

Typeset by Vision Typesetting, Manchester
Printed in Great Britain by
Anchor Brendon Ltd, Tiptree, Essex

for the publishers, B.T. Batsford Ltd,
4 Fitzhardinge Street, London, W1H 0AH.

Contents

Section E   Surface crochet

Acknowledgements

Without the help and co-operation of the following people this book would never have reached the publisher (and in fact nearly didn't). To Rita, a very special thank you. My grateful thanks also to: models Emily, Helen, Rita, Sue and Yvonne, who had to be revived with hot baths and various other hot liquids; the owners of Thurnham Hall, Mr and Mrs Crabtree, who fulfilled their agreement under great personal difficulty; Peter Hughes, who did such a marathon stint of photography with frozen fingers (although the frostbite does not show up in the results); Meryl and Karen for the checking, etc; Jane, Joan, Kathleen and Mary for the use of their garments for photography and Sue the beautician.

Thanks, in addition, go to Avon for the make-up and Pippa-dee for the accompanying garments.

Most of all I must thank all my students everywhere who have made the designs contained in this book possible. You were the ones who issued me with ultimatums and demands for designs out of the seemingly impossible, thus stretching me as I hope I stretched you.

Introduction

The Technique of Crochet is a book to be enjoyed. It has no rigid rules, only suggestions and guidelines. Its main aim is to highlight some of the areas of excitement and exploration which are possible with a crochet hook whilst at the same time keeping the limits of commonsense imposed by sound craft and design techniques. The book has attempted to inspire the reader to 'try' and not be afraid of trying.

Initially the basic stitches covered in the *Creative Design in Crochet*, Batsford Craft Paperback, have been quickly revised and more included. Each stitch has its own pattern which illustrates stitch and design techniques not covered in that first book.

Following this, we take a look at how shape can play a major role in design, with a simple geometric shape being used once for the main items or many times as motifs. Irregular shapes are also dealt with as these often require very skilful handling to keep the final items within the confines of the actual shape and form of the article.

A look at 'texture' means both the texture of the commercially available yarns and the texture that can be put into the crochet with a variety of stitch combinations.

The section on colour also includes how to work surface crochet onto different backgrounds, and encourages the reader to rid themselves of any reluctance or prejudices about using colour.

Finally, crochet is a useful craft to mix with others: both needlecrafts and some of the 'hard' crafts. Crochet is *fun* . . . see for yourself.

The Technique of
CROCHET

Section A
Using basic stitches

1. Slip knot

It is impossible to crochet without a loop on the hook. A slip knot is an effective way to commence crochet as it can easily be pulled back without any yarn wastage. Normally how the slip knot is made does not matter, but sometimes it is essential for the tail end of the yarn in the slip knot to be the thread that tightens the loop on the hook.

Diagram 1 Making a slip knot so that the tail end of yarn tightens the loop

The simple button pattern below depends on the *end* of the ball of yarn being the thread that adjusts the size of the loop. Diagram 1 shows how to make a slip knot in which the end makes the loop tighter or slacker (not the strand from the ball itself).

Simple button (Diagram 2)

To make

(Buttons are neater if worked on a smaller hook than the rest of the article being made.)

Make a slip knot that tightens when the end of a ball of yarn is pulled. Work 3 ch, slacken the first chain just above the slip knot and into this work 11 tr, join into a circle with a ss.

1 ch, 1 dc in each st to end. Break off leaving a 15 cm (6 in) length of yarn.

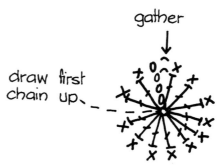

Diagram 2 Button

Fill the cavity with either a button or a washable toy filling.

Using a large-eyed sewing needle, sew a running stitch through all the double crochet stitches, gather tightly and fasten the gathers securely. Use the remainder of the yarn to attach the button to the article.

2. Chain and slip stitch

To make a chain (ch) commence with a slip knot on the hook. Yarn over hook (yoh), draw through the loop on hook – one chain made (see diagram 3).

Diagram 3 Making a chain

Chains are used: as a foundation to work other stitches into; to lift the hook to the correct height for the next row of stitches (i.e. a turning chain); to connect one part of the crochet work to another, creating spaces and lacy pattern effects.

A slip stitch (ss) is a chain anchored to another stitch. It has no height and therefore the hook does not need any chain to lift it. To make a slip stitch, simply place the hook into the crochet keeping the last loop of the last stitch on the hook in the normal way, yarn over hook, and draw through the crochet and the loop – one slip stitch made (see diagram 4).

Diagram 4　Slip stitch: the yarn is pulled straight through all loops

Slip stitches are used: to join rows into rounds to form tubes; to link rows when working in circles; to carry the yarn over a few stitches.

A picot can be made in lengths of chain to give interest to a basic net fabric. Using a fabric of 'five chains, join with slip stitch in five-chain space' (as in the overtop in Chapter II of *Creative Design in Crochet*), added detail can be achieved by working five chains, slip stitch to the third chain from hook, two chains, join into the five-chain space with a slip stitch (see diagram 5).

Diagram 5　Slip stitch to third chain from hook to make a picot

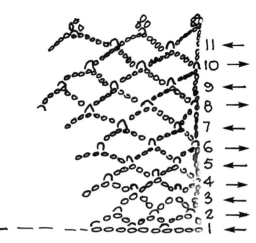

Diagram 6　Collar in chain and slip stitch

Collar using chain and slip stitch (Diagram 6, figure 1)

Size

Approximately 38 cm (15 in) neck with a 5 cm (2 in) depth.

Materials

1 ball Coat's No 10 mercerised cotton.
1.75 mm hook.
1 small button.

To make

Work 133 ch using the 1.75 mm hook.

Row 1 1 ss in 7th ch from hook, *3 ch, miss 2 ch, 1 ss in next ch, rep from * to end, 5 ch, turn. (43 sps)

Row 2 1 ss in first loop, *4 ch, 1 ss in next 3 ch loop, rep from * to end, 6 ch, turn.

Row 3 1 ss in first loop, *5 ch, 1 ss in next ch loop, rep from * to end, 6 ch, turn.

Row 4 As row 3 but turn with 7 ch.

Row 5 1 ss in first loop, *6 ch, 1 ss in next loop, rep from * to end, 7 ch, turn.

Row 6 As row 5 but turn with 8 ch.

Row 7 1 ss in first loop, *7 ch, 1 ss in next loop, rep from * to end, 8 ch, turn.

Row 8 As row 7 but turn with 9 ch.

Row 9 1 ss in first loop, *8 ch, 1 ss in next loop, rep from * to end, 9 ch, turn.

Row 10 As row 9 but turn with 7 ch, 1 ss in 4th ch from hook, 4 ch (1 picot made in centre of chain loop).

Row 11 1 ss in first loop, *4 ch, 1 ss in 4th ch from hook, 4 ch, 1 ss in next loop, rep from * to end. Fasten off.

Figure 1 Slip stitch and chain accessory

Neck edge

Rejoin yarn to starting ch, *5 ch, 1 ss in loop, rep from * to end.

Work a 5 ch loop as a buttonhole loop, with a ss in same places as last ss. Fasten off securely.

Sew a button onto the opposite side of the collar to correspond with button hole loop.

Variations

a Thin ribbon can be threaded through the neck edge loops.

b Thread 43 beads onto the yarn before starting the collar at all. During the last row draw up a bead to sit in the centre of the picots.

One historical use of the slip stitch was to make heavy beaded purses. The old British name of working a slip stitch through one strand only (usually the back loop) is 'single crochet', and it is this method of working that was adopted for the bead purses, pence jugs, etc. (Note: this is quite unlike the American single crochet.)

Beaded Thimble Case (Diagram 7, figure 2)

Materials

1 ball DMC No 10 mercerised cotton.

1.75 mm hook.

Pkt of Indian loom beads (approximately 90 will be required).

To make

Thread the beads onto the cotton before commencing the crochet. If there is difficulty getting the cotton through the bead, dip the end of the cotton into household glue. Roll the cotton into a tighter twist until the glue dries, then thread. The number of beads required will depend upon how many beads have been planned in the pattern. If the beading follows the crochet as stated in the pattern below, 75 beads are needed plus an extra 6 for the ends of the drawstring.

Diagram 7 Thimble case

Special note: the work is not joined and turned in this pattern but it is a continuous spiral! 3 ch, join with ss into a ring.

Work ss in the back loop only *throughout*. (2 ss in next ch) 3 times. Place a marker such as a safety pin at this point to show the start of the rows. (2 ss in next st, 1 ss) 3 times; (2 ss in next st, slide one bead down to the front, 1 ss in each of next 2 sts, 1 bead) 3 times; (2 ss in next st, 3 ss) 3 times; (2 ss in next st, 1 bead, 2 ss, 1 bead 2 ss, 1 bead) 3 times; (2 ss in next st, 5 ss) 3 times. It is a good idea at this point to darn in any long thread from the start of the circle. (2 ss in next st, 1 bead, 2 ss, 1 bead, 2 ss, 1 bead) 3 times. The work has no further increases. *24 ss, (1 bead, 2 ss) 12 times rep from * 3 times. 48 ss.

Next round (1 ss, miss 1 st, 2 ch) 12 times, join with ss, 36 ss. Fasten off. Check there are 6 beads still threaded onto the ball of yarn. Make a drawstring approximately 40 ch. Place 3 beads in the first chain, ss to last ch, before working last chain thread drawstring through chain spaces. 3 beads in the last chain. Fasten ends into drawstring securely.

Figure 2 Beaded thimble case

sc

3. Double crochet

To make double crochet (dc), commence with a line of chain (remember not to count the loop on the hook). Insert the hook under two strands of the third chain from hook, yarn over hook, draw through to the front of the work, yarn over hook, draw through the two loops on hook – one double crochet made (see diagram 8). Continue by placing one double crochet in each chain to the end. Lift the hook by working one turning chain. This counts as the first stitch. Turn work away from the body so the smooth side of the chain at the end of the row will be facing when the last st is worked.

Diagram 8 Double crochet

Double crochet is the easiest of all stitches to accidentally decrease at the end of a row. Until the double crochet fabric is very familiar, regular counting saves a lot of unnecessary pulling back.

See *Creative Design in Crochet* for decreasing; increasing in double crochet; double crochet rib and the Crab stitch.

Seamless raglan-style jacket
using only dc and ch (Diagram 9, figure 3)

Size
To fit size 91–97 cm (36–38 in)

Materials
800 g Jarol Aran yarn.
5.50 mm hook.

Tension
7 sts to 5 cm (2 in).

To make
Commencing at neck edge and using the 5.50 mm hook, work 57 chain loosely.

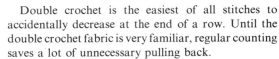

← start from neck

FOLD

Join each round

FOLD

front, back, front (132 sts)

Diagram 9 Seamless jacket in double crochet

Figure 3 *Double crochet classic for autumn*

Where the pattern says 'inc' place 2 dc in the *back loop only* of the same stitch. It is advisable to use safety pins as markers for the increases and as the work progresses move the pin nearer the edge.

Row 1 1 dc in 3rd chain from hook, 1 dc in each ch to end (56 sts).

Row 2 1 ch, turn, 9 dc, inc, 1 dc, inc, 2 dc, inc, 1 dc, inc, 20 dc, inc, 1 dc, inc, 2 dc, inc, 1 dc, inc, 10 dc.

Row 3 and all alternate rows, dc to end (commence with 1 ch for the first st).

Row 4 1 ch, turn, 10 dc, inc, 1 dc, inc, 4 dc, inc, 1 dc, inc, 22 dc, inc, 1 dc, inc, 4 dc, inc, 1 dc, inc, 11 dc.

Row 6 1 ch, turn, 11 dc, inc, 1 dc, inc, 6 dc, inc, 1 dc, inc, 24 dc, inc, 1 dc, inc, 6 dc, inc, 1 dc, inc, 12 dc.

Row 8 1 ch, turn, 12 dc, inc, 1 dc, inc, 8 dc, inc, 1 dc, inc, 26 dc, inc, 1 dc, inc, 8 dc, inc, 1 dc, inc, 13 dc.

Row 10 1 ch, turn, 13 dc, inc, 1 dc, inc, 10 dc, inc, 1 dc, inc, 28 dc, inc, 1 dc, inc, 10 dc, inc, 1 dc, inc, 14 dc.

Row 12 1 ch, turn, 14 dc, inc, 1 dc, inc, 12 dc, inc, 1 dc, inc, 30 dc, inc, 1 dc, inc, 12 dc, inc, 1 dc, inc, 15 dc.

Row 14 1 ch, turn, 15 dc, inc, 1 dc, inc, 14 dc, inc, 1 dc, inc, 32 dc, inc, 1 dc, inc, 14 dc, inc, 1 dc, inc, 16 dc.

Row 16 1 ch, turn, 16 dc, inc, 1 dc, inc, 16 dc, inc, 1 dc, inc, 34 dc, inc, 1 dc, inc, 16 dc, inc, 1 dc, inc, 17 dc.

Row 18 1 ch, turn, 17 dc, inc, 1 dc, inc, 18 dc, inc, 1 dc, inc, 36 dc, inc, 1 dc, inc, 18 dc, inc, 1 dc, inc, 18 dc.

Row 20 1 ch, turn, 18 dc, inc, 1 dc, inc, 20 dc, inc, 1 dc, inc, 38 dc, inc, 1 dc, inc, 20 dc, inc, 1 dc, inc, 19 dc.

Row 22 1 ch, turn, 19 dc, inc, 1 dc, inc, 22 dc, inc, 1 dc, inc, 40 dc, inc, 1 dc, inc, 22 dc, inc, 1 dc, inc, 20 dc.

Row 24 1 ch, turn, 20 dc, inc, 1 dc, inc, 24 dc, inc, 1 dc, inc, 42 dc, inc, 1 dc, inc, 24 dc, inc, 1 dc, inc, 21 dc.

Row 26 1 ch, turn, 23 dc, inc, 26 dc, inc, 48 dc, inc, 26 dc, inc, 24 dc.

Row 28 1 ch, turn, 21 dc, inc, 1 dc, inc, 28 dc, inc, 1 dc, inc, 44 dc, inc, 1 dc, inc, 28 dc, inc, 1 dc, inc, 22 dc.

Row 30 1 ch, turn, 24 dc, inc, 30 dc, inc, 50 dc, inc, 30 dc, inc, 25 dc.

Row 32 1 ch, turn, 22 dc, inc, 1 dc, inc, 32 dc, inc, 1 dc, inc, 46 dc, inc, 1 dc, inc, 32 dc, inc, 1 dc, inc, 23 dc.

Row 34 1 ch, turn, 25 dc, inc, 34 dc, inc, 52 dc, inc, 34 dc, inc, 26 dc.

Row 36 1 ch, turn, 23 dc, inc, 1 dc, inc, 36 dc, inc, 1 dc, inc, 48 dc, inc, 1 dc, inc, 36 dc, inc, 1 dc, inc, 24 dc.

Row 38 1 ch, turn, 27 dc, inc, 38 dc, inc, 54 dc, inc, 38 dc, inc, 27 dc.

Row 40 1 ch, turn, 24 dc, inc, 1 dc, inc, 40 dc, inc, 1 dc, inc, 50 dc, inc, 1 dc, inc, 40 dc, inc, 1 dc, inc, 25 dc.

Row 42 1 ch, turn, 28 dc, inc, 42 dc, inc, 56 dc, inc, 42 dc, inc, 28 dc.

Row 44 1 ch, turn, 25 dc, inc, 1 dc, inc, 44 dc, inc, 1 dc, inc, 52 dc, inc, 1 dc, inc, 44 dc, inc, 1 dc, inc, 26 dc.

Row 45 1 ch, turn, 28 dc, 10 ch, miss 50 sts, 54 dc, 10 ch, miss 50 sts, 29 dc, 1 ch, turn.

Work 52 rows on these 132 sts [made up of 1 ch to turn, plus 28, plus 10, plus 54, plus 10, plus 29]. Length can be adjusted here.

Border row *2 ch, anchor with ss on row below missing 2 sts, [an alternative is to anchor 2 rows below missing 1st], crochet 4 dc over 2 ch loop to bring hook back to top of work, 3 dc, (do not miss a st for the ch), rep from * 36 times, 1 dc in last st, 1 ch turn. (Diagram 10)

Next row Dc to end. Fasten off work.

Diagram 10 The two chains anchored in the work two rows below have no height or stitch increase, even when the four double crochets are added

Sleeves (seamless)

Join yarn to centre of 10 ch, 1 ch, 59 dc, 1 ss to join, 1 ch, turn.

Work 3 rnds dc joining each rnd with a ss and turning on each row.

Next rnd dc 2 tog, dc to last 2 sts, dc 2 tog, join with ss, 1 ch, turn.

Rep last 4 rnds 14 times (30 sts).

Work 7 rnd dc.

One rnd as border row of body.

One rnd dc.

Complete with one rnd Crab st (right side facing for this row).

Fasten off securely.

Work another sleeve to match.

Front and neck borders

With RS facing, commence at base of right front by joining in the yarn, 1 ch, *3 dc to 4 row ends (check border is flat), rep from * up front, 3 dc in corner st, 7 dc, dc 2 tog at front neck, 6 dc, dc 2 tog at back neck, 7 dc, dc 2 tog, 7 dc, dc 2 tog, 6 dc, dc 2 tog, 8 dc, 3 dc in corner st, *3 dc in 4 row ends, rep from * to base, 1 extra dc in last st, 1 ch, turn.

Next row: dc to end, 1 ch, turn.

Work border row once, dec 1 st over 2 at 4 neck corners, and place 2 extra dc in each of 2 front right angle neck points, 1 ch, turn.

Do not turn work as right side is facing, 1 row Crab st up front, round neck and down other front; carry on working Crab st along base edge of jacket.

Fasten off securely.

Variations

a Use a zip as a front fastener.

b Use the 'back loop only' stitches, which mark the shape of the raglan increasing, to create deeper texture by: *either* using 2 ch and ss to next back loop, *or* working 4 dc over 2 ch loops with a ss to anchor both ch and dc into.

4. Counterpane stitch

This is a variation on a double crochet. It is the same height as a half treble but does not require the yarn to be put over the hook first. To lengthen the double crochet, insert hook under two strands, yarn over hook, pull through to the front, yarn over hook, pull through *one loop only*, yarn over hook, pull through both loops – counterpane stitch made (diagram 11). Use two chains for turning.

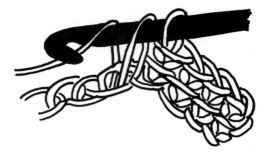

Diagram 11 Counterpane stitch has the same height as a half treble by working the first loop on hook once before putting yarn over and pulling through both loops

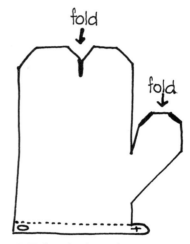

Diagram 12 Tailored mittens in counterpane stitch

Mittens using counterpane stitch
(Diagram 12, figure 4)

These mittens have a shaped thumb piece for comfort.

Size

To fit an average adult hand. They can be made smaller with a size less hook, larger with a size bigger hook.

Materials

2 balls soft pure wool Aran (50 g).

4.50 mm hook.

2 buttons.

Tension

5 sts to 4 cm (1½ in).

Figure 4 Textured body warmer in basket weave, with fully-fashioned mittens and a colourful lightweight mohair beret

To make

Make 28 ch.

Row 1 1 counterpane st (abbreviated to CP) in 4th ch from hook, 1 CP in each ch to end, 2 ch, turn.
Row 2 1 CP in each st to end, 2 ch, turn. (26 sts)
Rep row 2 three times.
Row 6 1 CP in same place as turning ch, 1 CP in each st to end, 2 ch, turn. (27 sts)
Row 7 1 CP in each st to last st, 2 CP in last st, 2 ch, turn. (28 sts)
Rep rows 6 & 7 once. (30 sts)

Thumb

1 CP in same place as turning ch, 6 CP, 2 CP in next st, 2 ch, turn. (10 sts)
Work 3 rows on these 10 sts.
Next row 3 CP, dec 1 CP over 2, 2 CP, dec 1 CP over 2, 2 ch, turn.
Last row (dec 1 CP over 2) 3 times. Fasten off.

Palm/Back

Rejoin yarn in the same stitch that the 2 CP of the thumb have been worked.
2 ch, 23 CP, 2 ch, turn.
Work a further 8 rows on these 24 sts.
Next row 9 CP (1 CP over 2) twice, 10 CP, 2 ch, turn.
Next row 8 CP (1 CP over 2) twice, 9 CP, 2 ch, turn.
Next row dec 1 CP over 2, 5 CP (1 CP over 2) twice, 6 CP, 1 CP over 2, 1 ch, turn.

Next row 1 CP over 2, 3 CP (1 CP over 2) twice, 4 CP, 1 CP over 2, 2 ch, turn.
Last row *1 CP over 2, rep from * to end. Fasten off.

Welt

Row 1 Rejoin yarn to foundation row at straight edge. 1 ch, 1 dc in each foundation ch picking up 1 loop, 5 ch.
Row 2 1 dc in 2nd ch from hook, 1 dc in each of 3 ch, dc to end, 1 ch, turn.
Row 3 1 dc in each st to last st, 2 dc in last st, 1 ch, turn.
Row 4 2 dc, 1 ch, miss st, dc to end, 1 ch, turn.
Row 5 1 dc in each st to last 2 sts, dec 1 dc over 2, 1 ch, turn.
Row 6 Dec 1 dc over 2, dc to end.
Row 7 Crab st back and continue round tab until side of mitt is reached. Fasten off.
Make another mitt exactly the same (purists may wish to reverse the working of the thumb, so that it is on the other side of the mitten). Sew up mittens checking that there is a left and a right hand mitt!
Sew on button to match buttonhole fastening.

Variations

a Work a raised treble rib instead of a buttoned dc welt.
b Put a surface crochet motif on the backs for colour, texture and added design features.

5. Solomon's knot

The fabric produced by Solomon's knot is open and lacy. There is no turning chain in the accepted sense of the term.

Fine cotton crochet during Queen Victoria's life attempted to copy the many beautiful and intricate laces that were produced using pillow lace bobbins, the sewing needle and tatting or netting shuttles. Solomon's knots were one of the ways devised to reproduce the effect that the netted lace gave. *Traditionally* the effect of Solomon's knots was in a diamond pattern and the two stages needed to anchor the work into this shape was called a Solomon's knot (SK) (see diagram 13). The turning required 1½ knots

Diagram 13 Traditional Solomon's knots

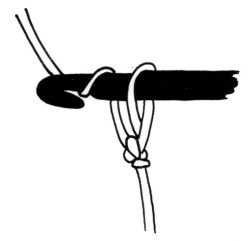

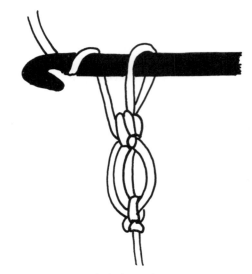

Diagram 14 (a) Extend chain. (b) Hook insertion

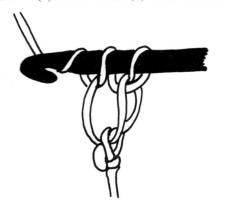

Diagram 15 Extend chain again

when using this definition. *Today* a Solomon's knot usually refers to just one stage, that is the ½ knot of Queen Victoria's time.

To make a SK, work a chain (just one) and extend this chain to the length required. The length depends on the thickness of the yarn and the hook size. As can be seen (diagrams 14a and 14b), the chain consists of a continuous loop and a single thread lying behind it. Insert the hook between the loop and the single thread (if you insert the hook anywhere else the whole chain will come undone). Yarn over hook, draw through to the front to have two loops on the hook, yarn over hook, draw through the two loops bringing the work back to a single loop on the hook (diagram 15). The foundation row could be a chain, or the stitches from previous work if SK is being used as an edging. However, on the whole it is better to use the knots themselves, to keep the soft open look from the very beginning. The number of SKs for the foundation row

depends upon whole length of the article being made (or the width – again depending upon the direction the SKs are being worked). These should be slightly longer than the chains being extended in the main body of the work; if not, the base row will be tight. If there is a difficulty to this stitch it is in trying to keep the extended loops an even size.

Once the foundation row has been made, there is a choice in the method of anchoring the next SK into the foundation row to form the diamond pattern.

First method: Add two more SKs for turning, work a double crochet into the centre of the third knot down from the hook. Continue along the foundation row by making two knots, and anchoring into the next foundation knot with a double crochet as before.

Second method: Work two more SKs as for the first method, but link the knots by working a double crochet in the chain before the 'knot' and a further double crochet in the chain after the 'knot'. This method makes the joining of the knots larger and more prominent than the first.

Both methods require three SKs to turn in order to keep the sides straight. Continue in this manner anchoring the next row into the pointed part containing a knot. To finish with a straight edge, it is necessary to work a row of extended SKs to match the foundation row (i.e. one knot longer than those in the diamond pattern of SKs, not two).

To work *horizontal* Solomon's knots, start with a foundation row of knots as before. Do not add any extra knots for turning but instead work the required

Diagram 16 Horizontal Solomon's knot

Materials
3 balls of contrasting George Picaud Chine No 1 mohair.
4.50 hook.

Tension
Really depends on you.

***Figure 5** Three-layer reversible scarf in Solomon's knots*

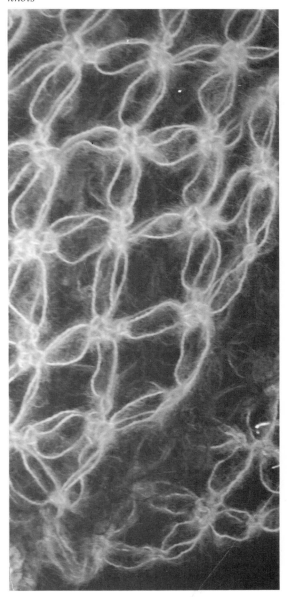

number of turning chain for the stitch chosen to link the horizontal rows to each other. For example, none for a slip stitch, one for a double crochet, two for a half treble, etc. (see stitch height page 41).

Having worked the turning chain, make an extended chain for a SK, connect this knot using the chosen stitch, placing one on either side of the chain's 'knot' (see diagram 16). The Knitting Craft Group have done an excellent leaflet on making colourful curtains using an advance technique to this method, entitled 'Spinnerama'.

Three-Layer Scarf (Diagram 17, figure 5)

Size (Approximation only)
90 × 30 cm (12 × 35 in) when stroked sideways to measure.

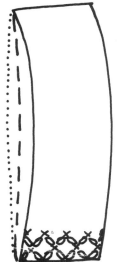

Diagram 17 Three-layered scarf in Solomon's knots

To make

Work 9 SK to form a foundation row of 7 longer length SK. The original scarf had the chain lifted by approximately 4 cm (1½ in).

Join the 9th SK to the 7th SK using the second method and lifting the remaining loops by 2.5–3 cm (1 in).

*Work 2 SK, join the next foundation knot, rep from * to end. Turn with 3 SK.

†Continue making rows of SK in a diamond pattern until the work measures 90 cm (35 in).

††Fasten off with a final row as described in the working methods above.

With a second ball (different colour), make the foundation row by joining yarn to the beginning of the foundation row made with the first colour. Join each knot to the knot of the first foundation row.

Work the remainder of this colour as a separate piece, unattached other than at the base, from † to ††.

Fasten off by connecting the final row to the first colour in the same way as the base row was joined.

With the third contrasting ball, work as given for the second colour. The sides are left open to give the wearer a choice of which colour is on the outside.

Variations

a Make larger sizes for luxury stoles, capes, etc., of extreme warmth.

b Wear it as a hood, cravat or body sash.

6. Trebles

The foundation chain needed for a straight edge using just trebles needs two more chains than the number of stitches required. To work the treble, yarn over hook, insert hook under two strands of the fourth chain, yarn over hook, draw yarn through to the front (three loops on hook), (yarn over hook, draw through two loops) twice, leaving one loop on hook on completion of stitch – one treble (tr) made (see diagrams 18a and 18b). One treble in each stitch to end. Lift the hook by working three chains before turning. 1 tr in each st to end. The last stitch is worked in the top of the turning chain. (If the fabric looks rather open at the turning chain edge, reduce the three chains to two chains.)

Increase by placing two stitches in the same stitch. If a very thick yarn such as rug wool is being used, make one stitch into the front loop only and the other into the back loop only.

Decrease (unless a special lacy pattern is being produced) by using two stitches of the row below to reduce to one stitch on the row being worked. That is,

work the first stitch until two loops are left on the hook, work the second stitch until three loops are left on the hook, yarn over hook, pull through all three loops (see diagram 19). (*Creative Design in Crochet* has other ways of using the treble.)

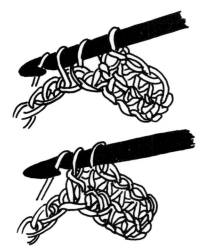

Diagram 18 (a) Yarn over hook before inserting into crochet. (b) Remove the loops on the hook, two at a time

Diagram 19 Decrease stitches by working into two stitch tops but leaving one loop of each stitch on the hook. Draw the last three loops together to form a decrease

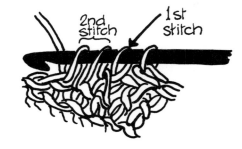

Casual Jacket (Diagram 20, figure 6)

Size

To fit bust 80–86 (88–96, 97–102) cm, 32–34 (34½–37½, 38–40) in.

Materials

Unconventionally the jacket uses two different yarns together. 400 g (450, 500 g) Wendy Donna worked with a contrast of Argyll's 4-ply Chevalier 200 g (250, 250 g). Any fluffy Aran thickness of one colour mixed with a fluffy 4-ply of the same fibre content can be substituted.

8.00 mm hook (tight crochet workers may need a 9.00 mm).

6 buttons.

Tension

7 sts to 9 cm (3½ in).

To make

Body

Using the 2 yarns together, work 87(97, 107) ch loosely.

Row 1 1 tr in 4th ch from hook, 1 tr in each ch to end, 3 ch, turn. (85[95, 105] sts)

Row 2 tr to end, 3 ch, turn.

Repeat row 2, 8 times.

Row 11 14 tr *tr 2 tog, 12(14, 16) tr, rep from * 4 times (80[90, 100 sts]) 3 ch, turn.

Repeat row 2, 8 times.

Row 20 14 tr, *tr 2 tog, 11(13, 15) tr, rep from * 4 times, 3 ch, turn. (75[85, 95 sts])

Work row 2 once.

Row 22 (first front), 18(21, 24) tr, 3 ch, turn. (19[22, 25] sts).

Repeat row 22, 12 times. Break off yarn.

Row 22a (Back) Join yarn to next st on row 22, 3 ch, 36(40, 44) tr, 3 ch, turn. Work a further 12 rows on these 37(41, 45) sts. Break off yarn.

Row 22b (Second front) Join yarn in next st of row 22, 3 ch, 18(21, 24) tr, 3 ch, turn. Work a further 12 rows on these 19(22, 25) sts. Break off yarn.

Join shoulders by double crochet on wrong side, using 11(13, 15) sts only of the fronts and from each side of the back.

Sleeves

(Both sleeves are made alike as there is no wrong or right side to crochet until it has been made to have a wrong or right side.)

Make 34 ch. This is the underarm seam as the fabric is worked round the arm and not from top to bottom.

Row 1 1 tr in 4th ch from hook, 1 tr in each st to end, 3 ch, turn. (32 sts)

Figure 6 *Easy-to-make full-sleeved jacket with pockets and fringed cravat*

Row 2 1 tr in each st to end. Repeat row 2, 24 times. Do not break off yarn but continue along the edges of these 26 rows to make the cuff.

Cuff

Row 1 1 ch, 1 dc in st top at end of every row (27 sts) – this gathers the sleeve. Add 4 ch for buttonhole tab.

Row 2 1 dc in 2nd ch from hook, 1 dc in each of next 2 ch, 1 dc in each st to end, 1 ch, turn.

Row 3 dc to last st, 2 dc in last st, 1 ch, turn.

Row 4 1 dc in same place as turning ch, 1 dc, 1 ch miss 1 st (buttonhole), * dc 2 tog, 6 dc, rep from * twice, dc 2 tog, 2 dc, 1 ch, turn.

Row 5 dc to last 2 sts, dec 1, 1 ch, turn.

Row 6 *dc 2 tog, 4 dc, rep from * 3 times, 1 dc. Break off yarn. Join underarm seam but not the cuff portion. Attach to armhole. Because there is no right or wrong side to the crochet check that the buttonhole tabs lie towards the back of the body.

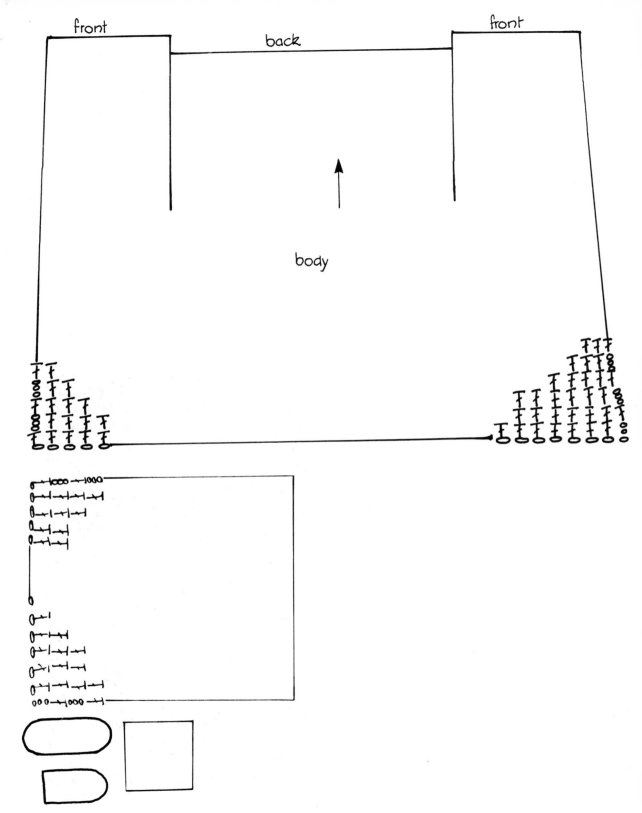

Diagram 20 Casual jacket in trebles

Collar

Join yarn to right front at the neck edge.

Row 1 1 ch, 1 dc in next 7(8, 9) sts, dec 1 dc over 2 using shoulder join as a st, 15 tr, dc 2 tog, 7(8, 9) dc, 1 ch, turn. Work 8 rows dc on these 30(32, 34) sts. Break off yarn. Rejoin yarn to base right front, 1 ch, dc up front using 3 dc to two treble row ends, place 5 dc up side of collar edge, 3 dc in corner, 1 dc in each stitch across top of collar, 3 dc in corner, 5 dc down edge of collar, dc to end down left front. Break off yarn.

Neck button tab

Row 1 4 ch, 1 dc in 2nd ch from hook, 1 dc in each ch to end, 1 ch, turn. (4 sts)

Row 2 1 dc in same place as turning ch, 2 dc (do not work in turning ch), 1 ch, turn.

Row 3 1 dc in same place as turning ch, 1 ch, miss 1 st, 1 dc, 1 ch, turn.

Work row 2, 4 times.*
Work row 3, once.
Work row 2, once. Do not break off yarn but work 1 row dc all round tab using 8 sts down each side and 1 st at each end (18 sts in all). This neatens and tightens the edges. Attach buttons at neck and cuffs.
Work two further tabs to *. Work row 2 twice. Fasten off. These are for the pockets.

Pockets

Work 14 ch.

Row 1 1 tr in 4th ch from hook, 1 tr in each st to end, 3 ch, turn.

Row 2 tr to end, 3 ch turn. Work a further 5 rows in tr.

Row 8 (Only turn with 1 ch) dc to end, 1 ch, turn.

Work 3 rows dc. Fasten off.

Attach tab to centre of pocket. Sew button on pocket to create gathers. Sew pocket to jacket.

Scarf Tie (optional)

9 ch, 1 tr in 4th ch from hook, 1 tr in each st to end, 3 ch, turn.

Work sufficient rows of tr to make an 80 cm length. To fringe: cut lengths of yarn approximately 13 cm (5 in) long. Double in two. Put loop end through st and pass the 2 ends through the loop. Pull tightly to secure. Fringe the edge of one side only for 27 rows but fringe both sides on the remaining rows.

Fringe end. Sew the straight edge to the shoulder (see figure 6).

Variations

a Work 2 rows dc on LH side. Evenly mark the position of the buttons with safety pins on the band. On RH side, 1 row dc, replacing 1 dc with 1 ch when a button marker is reached. Work a second row of dc to complete buttonhole band.

b Omit scarf and replace with a surface crochet motif on the LH side, between shoulder and bust lines.

Teenage square top (Diagram 21, figure 7)

The following pattern uses decreases to give a smooth line. Any badly worked decreases will show up as the design is based on the straight lines of a triangle.

Size

To fit chest/bust 71(76, 81) cm, 28(30, 32) in.

Tension

5 sts to 5 cm (2 in).

Figure 7 Shapes can produce a garment in themselves: a square forms a quick-to-make top with an optional design feature in making the square of two triangles

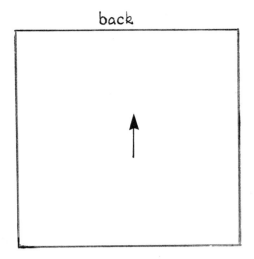

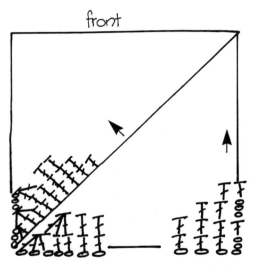

Diagram 21 Square top using rows of treble in different directions

Materials
125(125, 150 g) Foxstone Smoothie Tweed or any chunky, fluffy knit.
6.50 mm hook (tight crochet workers use a 7.00 mm).

To make
Back
Work 40(44,48) ch.
Row 1 1 tr in 4th ch from hook, 1 tr in each ch to end, 3 ch, turn. (38[42, 46] sts)
Row 2 tr to end, 3 ch, turn.
Repeat row 2, 20(22, 24) times. Break off yarn.

Front
Worked as a triangle to make one half of a square of the back and then the second triangle worked directly into the diagonal of the first triangle to complete the square. This is a design feature only.
(NB: When decreasing on a side in fashions, an extra chain is often needed to allow the garment to hang correctly.)
Make 40(44, 48) ch.
Row 1 1 tr in 4th ch from hook, 1 tr in each ch to end, 4 ch, turn.
Row 2 dec 1 tr over 2 (include the turning ch to count as a 2 tr decrease), tr to end, 3 ch, turn.
Row 3 tr to last 3 sts, 1 tr over last 3 sts, 4 ch, turn.
Repeat rows 2 and 3 until no sts remain. Then 20(22, 24) rows in all and the straight side should equal the length of the back.
Do not break off yarn but continue down the diagonal to work a second triangle.
Row A 3 ch, 2 tr in each tr row to end (the last tr should be at the edge of the work) 41(45, 49) sts, 4 ch, turn.
Row B tr 2 tog, tr to last 2 sts, tr 2 tog, 4 ch, turn.
Repeat row B 18(20, 22) times. (3 sts left)
Last row 3 ch, tr 2 tog.
Fasten off.
Join sides on wrong side with dc, leaving approximately 12 rows unconnected for the armhole. Join shoulder using 9 sts to each side of the back, and a corresponding amount on the front. If a slub yarn is used there is no need to crochet a final row as an edging, but if a smooth yarn has been used, work a row of dc and one of Crab stitch round armholes, neck and base.

Variations
a For beginners, this pattern can be worked in two squares using slightly less textured yarn.
b Place a drawstring through the last row of trebles to give a tight waist.

7. Textured trebles

To make a raised treble (Rtr), work a foundation row of trebles as described on page 24, section 6. Only two chains are required to turn as the hook is inserted lower down the fabric, round the stem part of the treble. (Remember the need for a turning chain is to lift the hook to the height of the next row.) By working round the treble stems instead of into the top of the treble stitch, the overall height of a raised treble fabric is shorter.

To make a raised treble that stands forward from the crochet, work a treble as normal but insert the hook from front to back at the right of the stitch being worked into and back to the front. This pushes the stitch to the front of that row. The abbreviation is RtrF (see diagram 22).

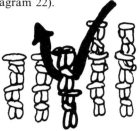

Diagram 22 Hook insertion for a raised treble at front of work (RtrF)

To make a raised treble that stands back from the crochet, work a treble but insert the hook from the back to the front, round the stem of the stitch being worked then to the back once more. It may be found easier if the crochet is bent slightly to allow the treble to be worked without catching the stitches of the crochet already made. This pushes the stitch to the back. The abbreviation is RtrB (see diagram 23).

Diagram 23 Hook insertion for a raised treble at back of work (RtrB)

Raised treble rib creates an elasticity within the crochet. The deeper the crochet rib (i.e. the further away from the foundation chain the work is) the more elastic is the result. A raised treble rib is *1RtrF, 1RtrB, repeating to end from *. Use two chains to

Diagram 24 Basket weave fabric produced using raised trebles

turn. All the stitches form ridges and it is important that these ridges remain in continuous lines. An alternative raised treble rib is 2RtrF, 2RtrB, repeating to end.

Raised trebles can be incorporated to create fabrics in the style of the knitted Aran sweaters (see *Creative Design in Crochet*, Ch. V). The following pattern for a body warmer uses the raised trebles to create a basket weave fabric (diagram 24).

Bodywarmer (unisex) (Diagram 25, figure 4)
Size
To fit bust/chest 81(91, 102, 112) cm, 32(36, 40, 44) in. Back length: 68 cm (27 in). (NB. There is no ease allowance to this garment as it is meant to hug the body for warmth.)

Materials
9(10, 11, 12) 100 g balls Lopi pure wool chunky. Hooks 9.00 mm, 6.50 mm and 5.50 mm.

Tension
5 sts in basket weave to 5 cm (2 in) using the 9.00 mm hook. (If the tension is too tight use a 10.00 mm hook.)

To make
Worked in one piece with no side seams.
With 9.00 mm hook, work 84(92, 104, 112) ch.
Row 1 1 tr in 4th ch from hook, 1 tr in each ch to end, 2 ch, turn. (82[90, 102, 110] sts)
Row 2 1RtrF, * 2RtrB, 2RtrF, rep from * to end, 2 ch, turn.
Repeat row 2, 6 times (11 cm [4½ in]).

Divide for side pocket slits
First front
Row 9 1RtrF, *2RtrB, 2RtrF, rep from * 3(4, 5, 5) times (2[2, 0, 2] st rem) 2RtrB if 2 sts rem, 2 ch, turn. (20[24, 26, 28] sts)
Work 9 rows in basket weave pattern (24 cm[9½ in]). Break off yarn.

Back
Rejoin yarn to next st of row 9, 2 ch.
Keep basket weave pattern and work 10 rows on 42(42, 50, 54) sts including turning chain. This leaves 20(24, 26, 28) sts for second front. Break off yarn.

Second front
Rejoin yarn to next st of row 9, 2 ch, work in basket weave on remaining sts for 10 rows. Break off yarn.
Rejoin yarn to top of 3 ch at beg of first front, 2 ch, work basket weave pattern over all three pieces for 10

rows. Length of work should now be approximately 38 cm (15 in).

Divide for right front
Next row 1RtrF, *2RtrB, 2RtrF rep from * until 18(22, 24, 26) sts have been worked. 2 ch, turn. Work 20 rows on these sts.
Next row ss over 6 sts, 2 ch to lift hook and continue to end in basket weave. Work a further 5 rows on these 12(16, 18, 20) sts. Break off yarn.

Back
Rejoin yarn into 5th st from R front and make 2 ch, (4 sts unworked).
Next row in basket weave work 23 rows on 38(38, 46, 50) sts. Break off yarn.

Left front
Rejoin yarn into 5th st from back by missing 4 sts and working 2 ch.
Work 20 rows on 18(22, 24, 26) sts.

Next row work 12(16, 18, 20) sts in basket weave, leaving 6 sts unworked.
Work a further 5 rows on these sts. Break off yarn. Join shoulder seams.

Pocket linings
Using 6.50 mm hook and with right side of work facing, join yarn to *back* of one of the side seam slits.
Put 16 dc evenly up the edge (this equals 3 sts to 2 row ends), 1 ch turn.
Next row 1 dc in each st to end, 1 ch, turn.
Rep this row 24 times, break off yarn.
Stitch this lining to the front section of the bodywarmer carefully, making sure the pocket lining does not pucker or show on the front.
Work another lining to match at the other side seam slit.

Armholes
The pocket lining will give you an opportunity to check that the double crochet lies flat against the basket weave stitch. If it has frilled, use less stitches per 2 rows for the armhole. If it has stretched slightly, use more stitches per 2 rows of armhole.
With right side of work facing and 6.50 mm hook, join yarn to underarm at centre.
1 ch, 1 dc in each of the 2 sts, dc round armhole using approximately 3 dc to 2 row ends, 2 dc to centre underarm, join with ss, 1 ch, turn.
Work 2 rows dc, dec 1 st at each underarm corner and one at shoulder (see *Creative Design in Crochet*, Chapter V for further details).

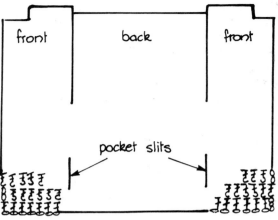

Diagram 25 Body warmer in basket weave

With right side facing, work 1 row Crab st. Fasten off. Work the other armhole to match.

Button band (left for a lady, right for a man)
By now the dc tension should be familiar and perfected.
Using the 6.50 mm hook and with the right side of the work facing, make approx. 85 dc evenly down edge of left front, 1 ch, turn.
Work 4 rows dc, break off yarn.
Using safety pins, mark the positions of the buttons.

Buttonhole band
Work as button band until 3 dc rows have been completed (including the first row worked into the main body)

Buttonhole row Work in dc until marker is reached when measured against the left front band, *at marker work 1 ch, miss 1 st, continue in dc to next marker, rep from * until all sts are used.
Work 1 row dc.

Neck band
With yarn joined to RH side of neck, at the corner, using a 6.50 mm hook, 1 ch, 3 dc across band, 5 dc across neck, dec 1 st over 2 sts round neck corner, 5 dc over shoulder, dec 1 st over 2, round back corner, 1 dc in each st across back neck, dec 1 st over 2 round back corner, 5 dc over shoulders, dec 1 st over 2 round neck corner, 5 dc across front neck, 4 dc across band, 1 ch, turn.
Work 1 row dc, 1 ch, turn.
Work 1 row dc decreasing 1 st at four corners of neck.
Rep last 2 rows once. Break off yarn.
Rejoin yarn to centre of back neck.
With 5.5 mm hook and right side of work facing, work

Crab st round neck, down right front, across base of jacket, up left front, round neck to centre back, join with ss. Break off yarn.
Sew on buttons to match buttonholes.

Variations

a Work only 1 row dc and 1 row Crab st for the front borders (adjusting the neck stitches as necessary) and replace buttons with a zip.

b Omit the armholes and work a square sleeve to change body warmer into a jacket.

Another way to create texture using trebles in crochet is to place many trebles in one stitch, but make sure there is only one chain left to work into on the next row. One way of achieving this is to place five or six trebles in one stitch and then bending them into a ring or tube as with the Popcorn stitch (*Creative Design in Crochet*, page 41). Alternatively a number of unfinished trebles can be worked into a stitch and then completed by putting yarn over hook and pulling through all the loops on the hook to give just one chain top for the next row. This is usually called a cluster and the pattern for the tea cosy below uses this latter method. The pattern also includes the use of curlycue tassels. These are made on the principle of increasing. If a large number of stitches are worked in the same place – and each subsequent stitch repeats the same thing – the stitches jostle for position which will give a deep waving or frilling in a solid fabric, or twist themselves into spirals if worked directly into the chain, to form tassels.

Tea cosy (Diagram 26, figure 8)

Materials

For large tea pot: 2×50 g balls chunky wool main; 2×50 g balls chunky in contrast.
6.00 mm hook.
Oddments for tassels.
For average/small tea pot: 2×50 g DK in main; 1×50 g DK in contrast.
4.50 mm crochet hook.

To make

Using either the 6.00 mm hook and chunky yarn, or the 4.50 mm hook and DK yarn, work 30 ch in main (M) colour.
Row 1 1 dc in 3rd ch from hook, 1 dc in each ch to end (29 sts), 1 ch, turn. Work 2 rows M in dc, changing to contrast (C) before completing last dc, to avoid a colour drag.

Figure 8 *Textured cosy for added insulation*

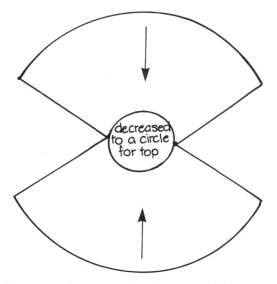

Diagram 26 Tea cosy using clusters and curlycues

Row 4 1 ch, *3 tr cl, 1 dc, rep from * to end, 1 ch, turn. (NB. If the clusters seem a little flat and not pronounced as the picture, either use a ss instead of a dc OR put 4 unfinished trs into the stitch instead of 3.)
Row 5 dc to end changing to M before last st is completed.
Work 2 rows dc in M. Change yarn before last dc is completed.
Work the last four rows 4 times more. Break off the yarn.
Work another piece the same but do not break off the yarn.
Keeping to M throughout, work across both pieces as follows: 1 ch, 1 dc in each st to end. (58 sts)
Continue round the circle in a spiral without joining and without turning work. Mark the start of the spiral with a safety pin. This changes the look of the dc. Continue over these sts once more (2 rounds worked). (dc 2 tog) 29 times (29 sts). Work 1 round dc. (dc 2 tog) 14 times, 1 dc. Work 1 round dc. (dc 2 tog) 7 times, 1 dc, leave a long thread and gather the remaining sts into a tight circle. Use the remaining yarn to attach the tassels.

Curlycues (tassels)

Make 9 ch, into 3rd ch from hook put 7 tr, work 7 tr into each of the rem 6 ch. Fasten off. Attach these to the tea cosy. The number of tassels/pom-poms or curlycues worked is up to you.
Join the edges of the cosy leaving room for the handle on one side and the spout on the other.

8. Long trebles

These are trebles that have the yarn wrapped round the hook more than once before inserting the hook into the work. These loops are then removed (by putting yarn over hook and drawing yarn through two loops). Repeat the action in the brackets until only one loop remains on the hook.

Diagram 27 Double treble has yarn placed twice round hook before inserting into crochet

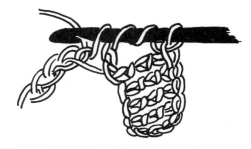

Diagram 28 Triple treble has yarn placed three times round hook before inserting into crochet

Diagram 29 Quadruple treble has yarn placed four times round hook before inserting into crochet

The most commonly used long trebles are:
  double treble (dtr), needing four chains to turn (diagram 27);
  triple treble (trtr), needing five chains to turn (diagram 28);
  quadruple treble (quadtr), needing six chains to turn (diagram 29).

Long trebles are particularly useful for:

a use as a carrier thread if added at the side seams or on a waistline for belts;

b allowing ribbons and ties to be threaded through as part of the design fabric;

c to be used as encroaching stitches (see Section D – colour);

d for texture when mixed with short stitches. The long stitches buckle to the size of the short ones, so creating texture.

The following sweater is based on this last principle.

Textured (unisex) sweater (Diagram 30, figure 9)

Size

To fit bust/chest 86/91 (97/102, 107/112) cm, 34/36(38/40, 42/44) in; length of body 60 cm (23½ in); length of sleeve 43 cm (17 in).

Adjust length of body or sleeve at † if necessary.

Materials

800 g (900 g, 950 g) Forsell Special Breed Pure Wool Jacob, Aran thickness.

5.50 mm crochet hook.

Tension

4 sts in pattern to 3 cm (10 sts to 3 in), 4 rows to 3.75 cm (just fractionally less than 1½ in).

To make

Body

Work 69(75, 83) ch.

Row 1 1 tr in 4th ch from hook, 1 tr in each ch to end, 1 ch, turn. (67[73, 81] sts)

Row 2 dc to end, 3 ch, turn.

Row 3 tr to end, turn (no turning chain required).

Row 4 *1 tr, 1 ss, 1 dtr, 1 ss, rep from * to last 2 sts (larger sizes to end), 1 tr, 1 ss, 3 ch, turn.

Row 5 tr to end, 1 ch, turn.

Repeat rows 2–5, 13 times (approximate length 53 cm [21 in]). † Work row 2 once.

Break off yarn.

Use the first foundation row to commence a raised treble rib as follows. Join in yarn to base of crochet, right side facing. 2 ch, *1 RtrF round stem of treble of foundation row, 1 RtrB round next stem of tr of foundation row, rep from * to end, 2 ch, turn.

Work 7 more rows in raised trebles keeping the ridges in rows.

Make another piece to match.

Join the two pieces on the wrong side at the shoulders leaving the central 36 sts unjoined as an opening for the slit neck. Do not join side seams.

Work 1 row dc followed by 1 row Crab st round the neck (have RS facing for the last row). Fasten off yarn.

Sleeves (all sizes)

Make 47 ch.

Row 1 1 tr in 4th ch from hook, 1 tr in each ch to end, 1 ch, turn. (45 sts)

†Work rows 2–5 of body once. The length can be increased by working extra patterns or shortened by omitting the first 4 rows.

Inc one st at beginning of *every* row until there are 77 sts. As the patt rows are repeated 8 times for length, the width at this point should be between 51–61 cm (22–24 in). Break off yarn.

Diagram 30 Textured unisex sweater using raised treble rib and bouclé stitch

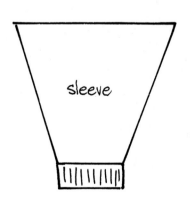

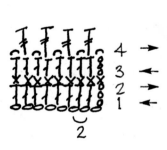

Figure 9 *Textured unisex sweater using raised treble rib and boucle stitch*

(NB: The bobbles should lie on top of each other as for the body pieces.)

Fasten off yarn and rejoin to foundation row as for body and work 7 rows raised treble rib in all. Break off yarn.

Work another sleeve exactly the same.

Attach sleeves to body using safety pins to keep in position. Check carefully that the sleeves are accurately placed to match each side so the same number of rows at the side seams are left. It is worth time and effort at this point! With wrong side of work facing, join the underarm sleeve seam and the side seam all in one. Fasten off.

Variations

a Omit bobble row and replace with a dc row for a plain sweater.

b Omit bobble row as above but work alternative rows at yoke in bobbles for a textured yoke effect.

c Work 1 of the body pieces in two parts (half the number of stitches), and add a 2 row dc band on each side to wear as a jacket.

Figure 10 *Section of a warm cape with surface crochet highlights (Kathleen Basford)*

Versatile cape/cloak (Diagram 31, figure 10)

This cape is based on long trebles with increasing and decreasing creating the pattern shape. The small amount of contrasting texture is produced by adding a little surface crochet (see Section E).

Materials

2×50 g balls of the following shades of Wendy Shetland DK: (A) Orthello, (B) Skye, (C) Westray, (D) Lerwick and (E) Stronsay; 1 ball of (F) White Heather; 3×25 g balls Wendy Amalfi mohair in Margharita.

4.50 mm crochet hook.

Tension

Not a crucial factor, but approximately 8 sts to 5 cm (2 in).

To make

With colour (C):

Work 94 ch, 1 tr in 6th ch from hook *1 ch, miss next ch, tr in next ch, rep from * to end, 1 ch, turn.

Row 2 dc to end, 4 ch, turn (91 sts)

Row 3 1 dtr in same place as turning ch, *1 ch, miss

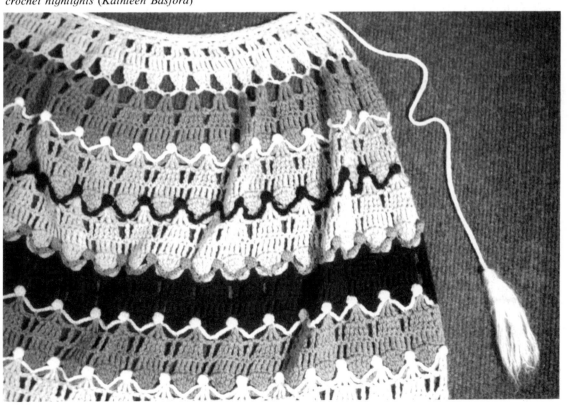

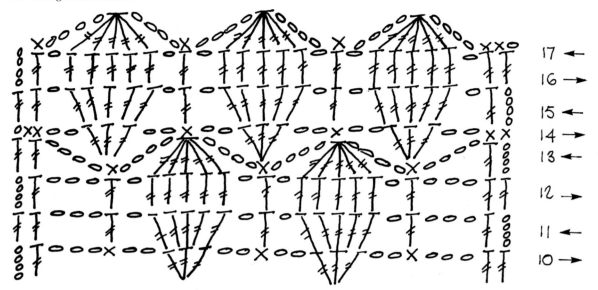

Diagram 31 Cape/Cloak worked in long trebles with surface crochet for emphasis

2 sts, 3 dtr in next st, rep from * to last 3 sts, 1 ch, 2 dtr in last st, 4 ch, turn. (29 groups)

Row 4 1 dtr, *1 ch, miss 1 ch, 1 dtr in next st, 1 dtr bet st just worked and next st, 1 dtr bet next 2 sts, 1 dtr in last st of group, rep from * to last 3 sts, 1 ch, miss 1 ch, 2 dtr, 4 ch, turn.

Row 5 1 dtr, *5 ch, 4 dtr cl using each st of group, rep from * to last 2 sts, 5 ch, 2 dtr. Change to colour (E): 4 ch, turn.

Row 6 1 dtr, 2 ch, miss 2 ch, 3 dtr in next ch, *3 ch, miss 5 sts, 3 dtr in centre chain, rep from * to last 4 sts, 2 ch, 2 dtr, 4 ch, turn. (30 groups)

Row 7 1 dtr, 1 ch, miss 2 ch, *1 dtr on dtr, (1 dtr bet dtrs, 1 dtr on dtr) twice, 1 ch, miss 2 ch, rep from * to last 4 sts, 1 ch, miss 2 ch, 2 dtr, 4 ch, turn.

Row 8 1 dtr, 1 ch, miss 1 ch, *5 dtr, 3 ch, miss 1 ch, rep from * to last 3 sts, 1 ch, miss 1 ch, 2 dtr, 1 ch, turn.

Row 9 1 dc in same place as ch, 1 dc, 4 ch, miss 2 ch, *5 dtr cl, 4 ch, miss 1 ch, 1 dc in next ch, 1 ch, miss 1 ch, rep from * to last 2 sts, 2 dc. Change to colour (B): 4 ch, turn.

These 9 rows form the foundation and increase for the shoulders and should measure approximately 15 cm (6 in) in length. The next 8 rows form the pattern, changing colour on every 5th row.

Row 10 1 dtr, 3 ch, 1 dc in cl top, 3 ch, *3 dtr in dc, 3 ch, 1 dc in cl, 3 ch, rep from * to last 2 sts, 2 dtr, 4 ch, turn.

Row 11 1 dtr, 3 ch, 1 dtr on dc, *1 ch, 1 dtr on first dtr, (1 dtr bet sts, 1 dtr on dtr) twice, 1 ch, 1 dtr on dc, rep from * to last 5 sts, 1 ch, miss 3 ch, 2 dtr, 4 ch, turn.

Row 12 1 dtr, 3 ch, 1 dtr on dtr, *1 ch, 5 dtr, 1 ch, 1 dtr on dtr, rep from * to last 5 sts, 3 ch, miss 3 ch, 2 dtr, 4 ch, turn.

Row 13 1 dtr, *4 ch, 1 dc on dtr, 5 dtr cl, 4 ch, rep from * to last 7 sts, 1 dc on dtr, 4 ch, miss 3 ch, 2 dtr, change to colour (D), 1 ch, turn.

Row 14 1 dc in same place as turning ch, 1 dc, 2 ch, *3 dtr in dc, 2 ch, 1 dc in cl, 2 ch, rep from * to last 6 sts, 2 ch, miss 4 ch, 2 dc, 4 ch, turn.

Row 15 *1 dtr, 1 ch, 1 dtr, (1 dtr bet sts, 1 dtr on st) twice, 1 ch, rep from * to last 2 sts, 2 dtr, 4 ch, turn.

Row 16 1 dtr, * 1 ch, 5 dtr, 1 ch, 1 dtr, rep from * to last st, 1 dtr, 1 ch, turn.

Row 17 1 dc in same place as turning ch, 1 dc, *4 ch, 5 dtr cl, 4 ch, 1 dc on dtr, rep from * to last st, 1 dc, change to colour (A), 4 ch, turn.

Repeat rows 10–17 inclusive, 3 times. Change colour at rows 13 and 17 in the following sequence. After (A) work with colour (E), then (C), (B), (D), (A) and (E).

Row 42 1 dtr in same place as turning ch, 1 ch, 1 dtr in next st, 1 ch, 1 dc in cl, 1 ch, *(1 dtr, 1 ch) 3 times in dc, 1 dc in cl, 1 ch, rep from * to last 6 sts, 1 dtr, 1 ch, 1 dtr in next dc, 1 dtr in last st, 1 ch, turn.

Row 43 1 dc, 3 ch, miss 3 sts, 1 dc in dc, *3 ch, 1 dc in central dtr, 3 ch, 1 dc in dc, rep from * to last 5 sts, 3 ch, 1 dc in last st. Break off yarn.

Fringe

Cut a piece of stiff card approximately 15 cm (6 in) long and wrap the mohair yarn round the card 5 times to give 10 strands in each fringe group. Cut along one edge of the card only and place the doubled edge into the 3 ch space. Pull the 10 ends through the loop and tighten.

Surface bobbles

For the method of working these bobbles see Section E, page 91.

The colour sequence is as follows:

Omit the base of row 5 of the foundation group and commence working the surface bobbles over row 9 with colour (F), then place the bobbles at the base of every pattern as shown in Diagram 31 using the colour sequence (A), (E), (C), (F), (A), (E), (F), (C).

Cord tie

Use 2 strands of colour (F) together and crochet a chain approximately $1\frac{1}{2}$ metres (60 in). Make two tassels by winding the mohair yarn over the stiff card 5 times, as if for the fringe. Attach one tassel securely to the end of the chain and thread the chain through the holes in the neck made by the 1 ch sp. Attach second tassel to other end.

Work all ends into the cloak neatly and trim fringe or tassels if necessary.

9. Half trebles

The half treble is the one stitch that does not follow the general rule and guidelines for producing an even crochet fabric. One of the main reasons is the construction of the top of the stitch. (Diagram 32.) Instead of there being two strands of yarn to form a chain look, it has three strands to give a double chain look. This gives the worker a choice of places to insert the hook. (For further information on the half treble, see chapter VII of *Creative Design in Crochet*.)

Below is a child's muff using the basic stitch.

Diagram 32 The half treble has yarn pulled through all three loops at the same time

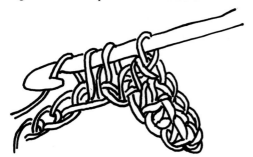

Child's muff (Diagram 33)

Size (before joining into a tube)
24 cm trimming edge × 28 cm ($9\frac{1}{2}$ in × 11 in).

Materials

1 ball Coney Chunky (or any 100 g ball of thick acrylic); 1 ball Smoothie (or any 25 g ball of brushed acrylic or other fluffy textured yarn of Aran to chunky thickness).
7.00 mm hook.

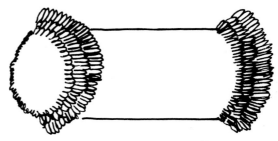

Diagram 33 Muff in half trebles with a three-layered edging

Tension

5 sts to 5 cm (2 in).

To make

With the Coney yarn and the 7.00 mm hook, work 29 ch.

Row 1 1 htr in 3rd ch from hook, 1 htr in each ch to end 2 ch, turn (28 sts).

Row 2 1 htr in same place as turning ch, 1 htr in each htr to end, omit working into the turning ch.

Work row 2, 12 times more. Break off yarn.

Borders (worked along the side of the htr fabric)
Join the textured yarn to one edge (there is no right or wrong side at this stage), 1 ch, 23 dc evenly down edge (this will work out at approximately 3 dc to 2 htr rows), 1 ch, turn.

Work a further 2 rows in dc. Fasten off.

Make another side border to match.

Join seam. This will be neater if the yarn for the border joins the borders and the yarn for the main part joins the main part.

Using 2 strands together make a chain long enough to go round the neck and attach to each end of the muff.

Variations

a Replace the border with a self-coloured border using htr Puff stitches. To make these, join yarn to side of muff, 2 ch, *1 htr in side of row, (yoh, place

Diagram 34 Direction of hook insertion before picking up yarn in a sideways half treble puff stitch

    hook in space behind htr just made, yoh, draw all loops up 2 cm [½ in]) 3 times, yoh, draw through all 7 loops on hook, 1 htr, rep from * to end. (See diagram 34.)

b Line the muff with a satin or smooth lining and sew 2 or 3 thicknesses of Courtelle wadding between the crochet and the lining. As the wadding is white it is often a good idea to encase the wadding between two pieces of lining (like a cushion pad) and then stitch it to the crochet on the inside.

Baby's hooded cape (Diagram 35)

Size
To fit a 6-month-old baby.

Materials
200 g Coney chunky yarn; 100 g of contrasting bouclé or slubbed DK yarn for the frill.
7.00 mm and 5.00 mm crochet hooks.

Tension
Using the chunky yarn and 7.00 mm hook, 5 htr to 5 cm (2 in).

To make
With chunky yarn and 7.00 mm crochet hook, make 15 ch for the hood.
Row 1 1 htr in 3rd ch from hook, 1 htr in each ch to end, 2 ch, turn. (14 sts)
Row 2 1 htr in same place as turning ch, htr to end, (omit working into the turning ch), 2 ch, turn.
Work row 2, 26 times more. Fasten off.
Fold in half. Join back of hood with a flat stitch. There should be no ridges or rough places to hurt the baby's head.

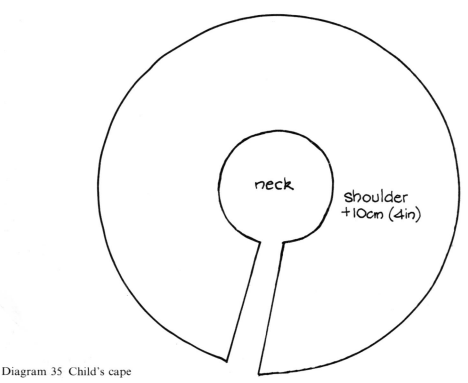

Diagram 35 Child's cape

Body

Make 22 ch.

Row 1 1 htr in 3rd ch from hook, 1 htr in each ch to end (21 sts), 2 ch, turn.

Row 2 1 htr in same place as turning ch, *2 htr, 2 htr in next st, rep from * 5 times, 2 htr, 2 ch, turn. (27 sts) Continue working the first htr in same place as turning ch.

Row 3 1 htr, *3 htr, 2 htr in next st, rep from * 5 times, 3 htr, 2 ch, turn. (34 sts)

Row 4 1 htr, *4 htr, 2 htr in next st, rep from * 5 times, 4 htr, 2 ch, turn. (41 sts)

Row 5 1 htr, *5 htr, 2 htr in next st, rep from * 5 times, 5 htr, 2 ch, turn. (48 sts)

Row 6 1 htr, *6 htr, 2 htr in next st, rep from * 5 times, 6 htr, 2 ch, turn. (55 sts)

Row 7 1 htr, *7 htr, 2 htr in next st, rep from * 5 times, 7 htr, 2 ch, turn. (62 sts)

Row 8 1 htr, *8 htr, 2 htr in next st, rep from * 5 times, 8 htr, 2 ch, turn. (69 sts)

Row 9 1 htr, *9 htr, 2 htr in next st, rep from * 5 times, 9 htr, 2 ch, turn. (76 sts)

Row 10 1 htr, *10 htr, 2 htr in next st, rep from * 5 times, 10 htr, 2 ch, turn. (83 sts)

Work 11 rows in htr without increasing. Leave the yarn attached. Sew the hood into place using a flat stitch and attaching the base of the first row and top of the last row to the neck opening. Return to the attached yarn and continue working htr from base of cape. 2 ch, and approximately 88 htr for the 2 fronts and round the hood (face edge). This works out at 5 htr for 2 htr row ends. Fasten off.

Border

With the contrast yarn and 5.00 mm crochet hook, join to right side of work at base of right front into the very front strand. (NB: Identify the 3 strands at the top of the stitches before commencing border.)

Into this front strand work 2 dc. Continue putting 2 dc in each st of front, hood, other front, and base. Join with a ss and fasten off neatly.

(NB: It is important to fasten off or the join will be noticeable.)

Into the middle strand, join yarn. Place 2 tr in each stitch around the border. Join with ss. Fasten off neatly.

Into the strand at the very back of the stitch work 2 dtr, continue until 2 dtr have been worked into each htr to the end. Complete with a ss and fasten off. Work a tie as given for the muff and add a tassel to each end after threading tie through the first row of htr of the body.

Variations

a Make an edging as described in **a** of the alternative ideas for the muff.

b Continue without further increases until length is suitable for a carrying or sleeping bag. Omit the fluffy yarn. Use a zip fastener up the front and close the hem, folding the crochet evenly so that the zip fastener is centrally placed.

10. Circles and tubes

Circles

Many shapes can be made from the circle by placing increases strategically to form various geometric outlines. Triangles, squares, hexagons, octagons, etc., can all be made from a ring of chain with a circle of stitches worked in the centre space of the ring.

The most important thing to remember when designing and working circles, or shapes made from a ring in the centre of that shape, is to increase by the same number of stitches on each round if using the same stitch throughout. It is the top of the stitch that determines whether the circle lies flat (i.e. the circumference), not the place where the hook is inserted.

A tension circle should be tried first to check whether the number of increases is correct. Unless very thin yarn is used on a big hook, or a thick yarn on a fine hook, the following is a useful guide.

Tension circle

Into a ring of 4 ch, joined with a ss:

Work 6 dc(8 htr/12 tr/24 dtr) join with ss,

1 ch(2 ch/3 ch/4 ch), turn work.

Increase on *each* row by 6 dc(8 htr/12 tr/24 dtr).

At the end of round 4 this gives

24 dc(32 htr/48 tr/96 dtr).

Unless following patterns (particularly from well-established firms in Britain and on the Continent), it is a good idea to turn the work on every round after joining with a ss. However, circular motif patterns on the whole do not tell you to turn the work and so the right side remains facing all the time.

Tubes

Many seamless items can be made from tubes. To keep the joining line of slipstitch and turning chain straight, it is necessary to turn the work on every row (see diagram 36). If this is not done the join will slant either

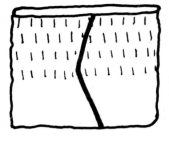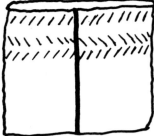

Diagram 36 (a) If work is not turned on each round, the joins on each round will have a bias in one direction or the other, depending upon the position of the first stitch. (b) Work turned on each round gives a straight joining seam

to the right or to the left of the first stitch. A very prominent slant to the left will occur if the usual stitch is worked into on each round (rnd) and the work not turned. A definite slant to the right will occur if the first stitch is worked in the same place as the turning chain and the work not turned.

One further point to consider when working in the round is that if the work is not turned on every round the look of the stitches will be quite different from the same stitches being worked in rows and turned in the normal manner.

The 1950's style of blouse uses a seamless tube for the body of the blouse to the underarm. Circular motifs are then joined and appliquéd to the front and back leaving sufficient motifs to act as an 'off-the-shoulder' blouse.

'1950-style' blouse (Diagram 37)

Size

Bust 82 (96) cm; 32 (38) in.
Length before motif: 32 cm (12½ in).
Length with motif: 36 cm (14 in).

Materials

3 (4) balls Tootal Cotton (10's thickness mercerized approximately 240 g [320 g]).
3.50 and 2.50 mm crochet hooks.
Shirring elastic (optional).

Tension

11 sts to 5 cm (2 in) on 3.50 mm hook.
Motif to 8 cm (3¼ in) diameter on 2.50 mm hook.

Body tube

With 3.50 mm hook make 168 ch. Join this chain

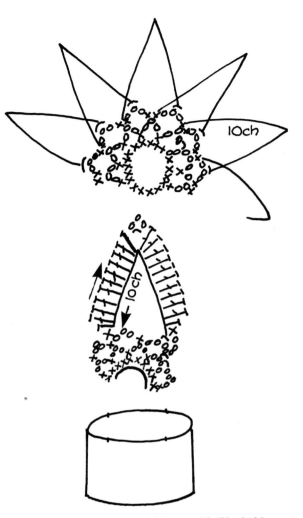

Diagram 37 (a) '1950 Style' blouse with 'V-stitch' pattern for body tube. (b) Diagram for motif using international signs

carefully with a ss into the first chain made so that there is a ring. Take definite precautions to avoid the chain twisting.

Rnd 1 3 ch, 1 tr in joining st of foundation ch, *miss 1 ch, 2 tr in next ch, rep from * to end, join with ss in centre of space made by 3 ch and first tr. (84 [100] 'V' sts) Because the ss is going into the space and not a stitch at the end of each round there is no need to turn the work.

Rnd 2 3 ch, 1 tr in same place, *2 tr in centre of next 2 tr (this pushes the trebles apart to form a 'V'), rep from * to end, ss to centre of first pair of sts.

Repeat round 2, 57 times. Work should measure 32 cm (12½ in). (Approximately 59 rows.)

Final rnd Work this round over one or two thicknesses of shirring elastic for added security: 1 ch, 1 dc in each st to end. Fasten off.

Motif

With 2.50 mm hook make 10 ch, join into a ring with ss.

Rnd 1 2 ch, 19 dc into ring, 1 ss into top of 2 ch.

Rnd 2 5 ch, *miss 1 st, 1 dc in next st, 3 ch, rep from * to end, join with ss to beg of round. Do not turn – 10 sps (*this is important*).

Rnd 3 It includes the petals. 3 ss to centre of 5 ch starting sp, 5 ch, 2 dc in next sp, 3 ch, 1 dc in next sp (the space just formed will anchor the subsequent following petal), 10 ch, put hook into the 5 ch sp made at the beg of round and make a ss. Now work over the 10 ch loop; in loop put 1 dc, 1 htr, 10 tr, a 3 ch picot, 10 tr, 1 htr, 1 dc, 1 dc in 3 ch sp that the 10 ch started from (this completes petal), 3 ch, 1 dc in next sp, 10 ch, ss this 10 ch to the 3 ch sp under the arch of the petal just made.

Continue making petals in this manner until 10 petals have been completed. Last petal fastened in 1 st 3 ch sp to the left of 1 st 10 ch, so it crosses over as other petals do.

Make a further 13 (15) motifs.

For convenience it is suggested that the petals of the motifs be sewn to the blouse and to each other. However, if you have worked with motifs before, you will probably find it a simple matter to join the motifs together during the last round; this provides the better finish.

Appliqué 3 petals to the body tube of 5 (6) motifs at the front and 5 (6) motifs at the back, leaving 2 motifs each side to slip over arms.

Variations

a Make the strip of circular motifs to fit the body tube exactly to make a strapless top. Include a ring of fine elastic to the inside of the tube whilst appliquéing the motifs to the outside.

b Work as **a** above. In addition make 2 short lengths of circular motifs as shoulder straps.

c Work as **a** above. In addition make a strip long enough to be appliquéd from the base of the left-hand side seam at a diagonal to the right shoulder; around the neck to form a halter-neck blouse; finally to form a matching diagonal from the left shoulder to the base of the right side seam, forming a cross in the centre of the bust line.

11. Shaping rows of crochet

One of the interesting aspects of crochet is the vast range of possibilities that are continuously available to those wishing to experiment and explore. Altering the regimentation of straight rows can be easily achieved either by increasing and decreasing within the same row, or by using the variety of stitch heights.

Chevrons are an excellent example of how a straight row can be bent into an undulating shape, using increases for the peaks and decreases for the depressions. (See page 65.) The dress on page 78 uses chevrons for the skirt and trims. As can be seen from the picture on page 78, coloured stripes respond well to this method of bending rows, creating a pleasing effect.

Many interesting patterns can be formed by the intelligent use of the various stitch heights. The waistcoat pattern below uses a variety of stitch heights to create 'waves'. Unshaped rows in contrasting colours are worked between the shaped rows but because of the shaping that has already taken place, the contrasting stripes 'bend'.

Another important use of creating shape with stitches of varying heights is in fashion crochet where a tailored effect is necessary. The human form is not a uniform shape. For instance, shoulders can be straight and broad or narrow and sloping, with any permutation in between and often with one shoulder quite different in length or position from the other. Any figure with sloping shoulders can have the fit of their garments improved by using the stitch heights to form a wedge-shaped row (or two rows) at the shoulders. A guideline to achieve this is to work the first quarter of the row nearest the armhole in ss, the next quarter in double crochet, the third quarter in half trebles with the remainder in trebles. (See diagram 38.) Obviously this can only be used if the fabric being crocheted is fairly firm and using simple, basic patterns. There are many ways to form similar shapings in more complex stitch patterns. The main point to remember is to make sure the dart or wedge is not too obvious. If an open lacy fabric is being created, it should not be necessary to make darts as these garments 'mould' to the body, finding their own fit.

The guideline given for the shoulder wedge above can be used to form a bust dart for the fuller figure, and a neck dart for a figure with a fuller back. Again let it be pointed out that shaping in the form of darts should not be included in any garment indiscriminately – only where the fabric pattern can incorporate it, and the figure shape warrants it. When working a bust dart the ss section of the row should be at the side seam edge.

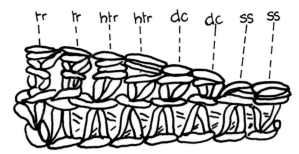

Diagram 38 Using stitch heights to create a shaped dart at shoulder

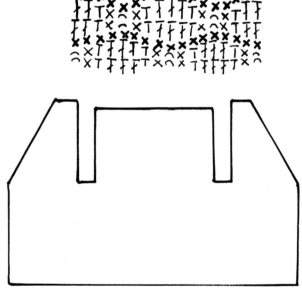

Diagram 39 Classic waistcoat using stitch height for fabric design detail

The dart shaping should take up less than one third of a row that is being worked across the body from side seam to side seam, and have stopped before the bust prominence. (For further information see page 77.)

Waistcoat (Diagram 39, figure 11)

Size Bust 76–81 (86/92–97/102) cm; 30–32 (34/36–38/40) in.

Materials

250 g (300 g/350 g/350 g) pure wool 4-ply in main colour; 1 ball (50 g) each of 3 contrasting colours. 3.50 mm and 4.50 mm crochet hook. 5 buttons.

Tension

1 pattern worked on 4.50 mm hook = 3.5 cm (1½ in).

Extra abbreviations

M = main colour; C1 = first contrast; C2 = second contrast; C3 = third contrast.

To make

Using 4.50 mm hook work 154 (170/186/202) ch in M.
Row 1 1 ss in 2nd ch from hook * 1 dc, 1 htr, 3 tr, 1 htr, 1 dc, 1 ss, rep from * to end (19[21/23/25] patts), no turning chain.
Row 2 *1 dc, 1 htr, 3 tr, 1 htr, 1 dc, 1 ss (each type of stitch should be on the same type of stitch of the row below) rep from * to end. (152[168/184/200] sts)
Row 3 With C1 1 ch, dc to end. Break off C1 yarn. Do not turn work.
Row 4 With M, 3 ch * 1 tr over dc, htr over htr, dc ss dc over 3 tr, htr over htr, 2 tr over dc and ss, rep from * to end, 3 ch turn.
Row 5 *1 tr, 1 htr, 1 dc, 1 ss, 1 dc, 1 htr, 2 tr, rep from * to end.
Row 6 With C2 1 ch, dc to end, break off C2. Do not turn work.
Row 7 *1 dc, 1 htr, 3 tr, 1 htr, 1 dc, 1 ss, rep from * to end, (no turning ch.)
Row 8 As row 2.
Row 9 With C3 dc to end. Break off C3. Do not turn work.
Rows 4 and 5 *and* 7 and 8 form the pattern by using stitch heights for shaping. The plain dc rows in colour are worked in sequence, i.e. C1, C2, C3, C1, C2, etc., with one band of colour between each two rows of main colour. Continue in this manner until 45 rows have been completed in all.

Figure 11 *Pleasingly patterned waistcoat obtained by varying the stitch heights*

First front

Work only on first 28(32/36/38) sts.

Decrease 1 st at front edge on *every* dc row until 16(16/20/20) sts remain (12[16/16/18] decreases). Continue until 52 rows have been worked from the armhole. Fasten off.

Back

Miss 19(19/19/23) sts for the under part of the armhole.

In M and with 4.50 mm hook continue keeping pattern straight. Work 45 rows on these 60(68/76/80) sts. This gives a single row in M to level the work. Break off yarn.

Second front

Miss 19(19/19/23) sts. Join in M. Keeping armhole edge straight and matching decreases at front edge to those of the first side; work in pattern on these 28(32/36/38) sts reducing to 16(16/20/20) sts. Work until 52 rows have been worked from armhole (the extra length on fronts is for the shoulder). Fasten off. Join shoulder seams matching stitch for stitch.

Armhole borders

Rejoin M to centre of an underarm, with RS facing and using a 4.50 mm hook put 90 dc evenly round armhole. Work 6 rows dc decreasing at shoulder and both sides of underarm points on every row, turn work after each row.

Work 1 row Crab stitch with RS facing and 3.50 mm hook. Fasten off.

Welt

Using the 3.50 mm hook work 10 rows of raised treble rib (see page 29). Fasten off.

Front and neck border

Rejoin M to base of right front with RS facing. Using 4.50 mm hook work 14 dc up welt, dc up front edge, 1 dc in each st across back neck, dc down left front, finishing with 14 dc in welt.

Work 3 rows dc decreasing 1 st at each side of back neck on every row.

Buttonhole row 1 ch, 2 dc *1 ch, miss 1 st, 11 dc rep from * 3 times, 1 ch, miss 1 st, continue in dc decreasing 1 st at each side of back neck.

Work a further two rows dc, decreasing at neck edge as before.

Change to 3.50 mm hook. Crab stitch round front and neck border.

Variations

a Use only one contrast which is a lighter or darker shade of the hue used.

b Make in one colour only. Add a little extra in the length. Reverse the fastenings, to make into gentleman's waistcoat.

Section B
Designs based on shapes

There is no magic to a designer's work, just a lot of hard self-application in the forms of observing, recording, analysing, experimenting *and* time, coupled with a persistent, patient perseverance.

If design is approached in a logical and basic way, building knowledge upon knowledge and experience already gained, the 'magic' stops being out of reach. So-called 'mysteries' can be explained and, with a bit of effort and personal application, come under control.

If it is any consolation to anyone, I was thrown out of the art class at the grammar school and placed in the music option (which I thoroughly enjoyed) so for years my mind believed there was no creative or artistic ability in my make-up. So let those who say 'I could never design' embark on the rest of this book with an open mind and a feeling of adventure. Allow yourself to explore your own potential, adding to your experience and knowledge and thereby triggering off your own ideas and creativity. The results will amaze and stimulate you.

First let us look at different shapes, their advantages and disadvantages. At the same time let us look at the use of each shape both on a large and a small scale.

1. Squares

A square as a piece of crochet fabric can be obtained in many different ways:

a Straight rows of equal length with the work being stopped when the length equals the width. This square of crochet can be used either sideways or in the direction it was worked (i.e. from bottom to top).

b Working two right angled (90°) equal triangles that together make a square. The triangles can be started:

(i) at the point of the right angle and increased equally on both sides;

(ii) at one of the equal sides and decreased at one side only;

(iii) at one of the two equal angle points and increased on one side only;

(iv) at the hypoteneuse (long side) opposite the right angle and decreased at one side only.

c From the centre using the principle of a circle to keep it flat as in the familiar 'granny' square (see page 46).

Points to watch for when making squares

1) The tension of the first two rows can be slacker than the rest of the square. In a garment where these two rows are often on the hip line it is not a bad thing to leave it if it does happen, but on the whole this possible failing has to be checked either by using a smaller hook after the chain, or consciously watching and gently tightening the tension during the first row.

2) If the first row lacks elasticity at the edge, this usually means the chain is too tight. Learning to make slacker chains is the best remedy, as habitually working tight chains will also make lacy patterns buckle and pucker. However, a larger hook *can* be a substitute answer for the working of the foundation chain as a last resort.

3) Working squares from point to point will give a bias and it will be difficult (although not impossible) to work a border that pulls it back into a perfect square.

4) When using square motifs to make a square item it may be necessary to pin out each square and lightly damp press (depending upon the yarn) to ensure that they are all the same size before joining them together.

5) If increasing or decreasing is used to shape work into a square, there should be no holes or uneven

edges – such as steps in the fabric – unless it is a design feature, otherwise the joins will be noticeable and ugly.

6) Working squares from the centre can cause a leaning bias to one side. Turning the work on every round should correct this tendency.

Items that can be made with squares

These include bags, cushions, knee rugs, sleeveless tops, shawls, and tablecloths.

The top on page 28 has one side worked in straight rows as one simple square (**a** above). The other side is worked in two triangles. The first triangle as **b**(ii) above with the second triangle using the long side of the first triangle for the first row (**b**(iv) above). This avoids a join across the centre of the body. It also has the crochet worked in two different directions giving it a simple design feature.

Smaller versions of the square can, of course, be used to make a patchwork; being joined together to form a complete whole.

Interesting effects can be achieved by varying the make-up of alternate squares. Or by joining one square which has been worked top to bottom to a square which has been worked in the same way, but placed with the rows side to side. Any textured stitch that emphasises the rows as straight lines should enhance and strengthen this effect.

Tension square

It is worth remembering at this point that for any practical article, the shape, size and overall fit will ultimately have to be controlled. Where the item is worked in rows, a tension square is advised so that the number of stitches can be worked out *before* a large project is started. Otherwise time and effort is wasted and then frustration sets in.

Granny or Afghan squares (diagram 40, figure 12)

These popular square motifs can be in one colour only or each row can be a different colour. The size of them is entirely up to you, 3, 4 or 5 rows being the average.

To make

(Hook size relates to the thickness of the yarn.)
4 ch, join with a ss.
Round 1 3 ch, 2 tr in centre of ring * 1 ch, 3 tr, rep from * twice, 1 ch, join to top of turning ch with a ss.
Round 2 If working in one colour 3 ch, turn (this leaves you over a space to work back along the next round). If using colour oddments, fasten off each colour securely and rejoin into next space with the new ball.

Figure 12 *Traditional knee rug in 'granny square' motifs. (Worked by J. Hadwin)*

Diagram 40 Stitch structure of a granny square

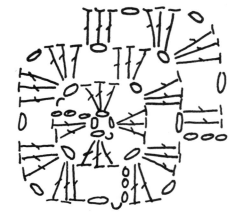

There is no need to turn the work if each row is finished.

Attach yarn to any sp. Work 3 ch, 2 tr, 1 ch, 3 tr, 1 ch in that sp; * 3 tr, 1 ch, 3 tr, 1 ch in next sp; rep from * twice; ss to top of turning ch.

Round 3 Attach new colour to any side sp. Work 3 ch, 2 tr, 1 ch in that sp; * 3 tr, 1 ch, 3 tr, 1 ch in next sp (corner); 3 tr, 1 ch in next sp (side); rep from * twice; 3 tr, 1 ch, 3 tr, 1 ch in last sp; ss to top of turning ch.

Round 4 and subsequent rounds Join yarn to any side sp that lies immediately before a corner sp. Work 3 ch, 1 tr, 1 ch in that sp; * 3 tr, 1 ch, 3 tr, 1 ch in next space (corner); 3 tr, 1 ch in each side sp; rep from * twice; 3 tr, 1 ch, 3 tr, 1 ch in last corner sp; 3 tr, 1 ch in each remaining side sp; ss to top of turning ch. Fasten off. To join squares together to form a larger fabric, see page 56.

2. Oblongs

Oblongs are rectangles (a shape with 4 right angles) that have adjacent sides unequal. In other words, a square that is stretched in one direction. As with the square, there are many different ways of obtaining an oblong.

a Work straight rows of equal length stopping before the length equals the width, or continuing the crochet for some distance after the work equals the width.

b Make two right-angled triangles with the other two angles being a different measurement. This gives two unequal sides to the triangle. The direction in

which the crochet is worked to obtain the triangle is a matter of choice. (See **b** on page 28.)

c Add a border to a square making the width of the top and bottom borders deeper than those at the side.

Points to watch for when making an oblong are the same as those for squares (see page 45).

Items that can be made with oblongs

They include scarves, bags, household covers, book covers, T-shaped tops, tabards, and rugs.

The winter sweater below has an oblong for its main section. A centre slit for the neck, gathering into the cuffs and a close-fitting mid-riff band complete the design of the sweater.

Short winter sweater (Diagram 41, figure 13)

Size

One set of figures fits any size from 75–100 cm (30–39 in).

The mid-riff section has a choice of sizes.

Materials

400 g Wendy Donna in a pale neutral tone; 3 differently coloured balls of 4-ply, ideally in dark or vibrant hues.

9.00 mm and 7.00 mm hooks.

Tension

4 sts to 5 cm (2 in).

To make

First grade the colours of 4-ply into A, B and C contrasts. A is over the bust prominence and C is across the shoulder.

Using 1 ball of the main colour (M) together with contrast A, make 92 ch with the 9.00 mm hook.

Diagram 41 Waist-length winter sweater

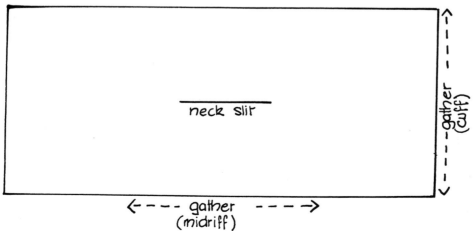

Figure 13 *Rectangular short-waisted jumper with emphasis on colour toning*

Row 1 1 tr in 4th ch from hook (check stitches are not inflexible – a large hook is best held further down the hook away from the hook head), 1 tr in each ch to end, 3 ch turn. (90 sts)
Row 2 1 tr in each st to end, 3 ch, turn.
Repeat row 2, 6 times.
Break off contrast A but keep M attached.
Join in contrast B. Work row 2, 6 times (14 rows in all).
Break off contrast B.
Join in contrast C. Work row 2, 4 times.

To avoid a shoulder seam join, and as the trebles in a fluffy yarn do not look unsightly if the back is worked downwards while the front is worked upwards, continue working in M and contrast C.
Neck row 3 ch, 32 tr, 24 ch, miss 24 sts, 33 tr, 3 ch, turn.
Next row tr to end working into each st and each chain. Work row 2, 3 times. Break off contrast C.
Join in contrast B. Work row 2, 6 times. Break off contrast B.
Join in contrast A. Work row 2, 8 times. Break off both yarns.

Welt

The easiest way to find out how many stitches are needed for the welt is to slip the neck slit over the shoulders. Place a safety-pin under each arm where the side of the body is. Remove oblong. Check there is an equal number of stitches on either side (the one in the photograph used 28 sts to join underarm and left 34 sts free at front and back for the welt).

Join underarm seams.

With 7.00 mm hook, join the main yarn to a side seam, 3 ch, 1 tr in each st to end.

Work 10 rows raised treble rib. Fasten off.

Cuffs

With 7.00 mm hook join yarn to underarm seam at cuff.

To gather the oblong into the cuff, place 1 tr into each row end.

3 ch, *tr 2 tog, 1 tr, rep from * to end, ss in sp between turning ch and 1st dec.

This reduces 37 rows at the 2 ends of the oblong to 26 sts, 2 ch, turn.

Work 10 rows raised treble rib.

Work the other cuff the same.

Neck edge

Because of the heavy texture of the yarn it is not necessary to crochet round the neck edge; however, 1 row of dc is a useful addition.

Should a smooth yarn be used work 1 row Crab stitch on top of the row of dc.

Smaller oblongs

These can be strips of crochet or another material such as leather, knitting or fabric.

Figure 14 shows oblong pieces of suede crocheted together to form a classic waistcoat. The crochet stitches are used to shape and give a good fit to the finished garment. Holes have been punched into each oblong of suede so that the yarn can be crocheted directly into the suede. (See page 112 for further information on using suede, leather and sheepskin in crochet.)

3. Triangles

Triangles like all shapes, can be produced in crochet by different approaches.

a In straight rows working from one of the three sides and decreasing to a point.

b Starting at a point and increasing until the correct length and width is reached.

c Starting in the centre as though for a circle and increasing in the same three places on each row.

Points to watch for when making triangles

1) When decreasing it is important that two stitches are drawn together as one so that there is a smooth edge.

   Do not miss a stitch in the decrease or this will leave either an edging of steps if the last stitch is missed, or an edging of holes if the next to the last stitch is missed.

2) It may be necessary to add on extra turning chain at the edges. The sides of triangles slope, covering more distance than a vertical line. The sides of the triangles may get tight unless an extra chain is added for ease.

3) When working triangles from the centre the points often become rounded rather than sharp. On the last row it helps to add a taller stitch in the centre of the group of increases at the corners.

Items that can be made with triangles

They include bikinis, shawls, yoke inserts, hair coverings (snood, headscarf), or a 'gypsy-look' skirt/top.

Mediterranean-style head cover (Diagram 42)

Size

53–61 cm (21–23 in) round head.

Materials

100 g lightweight slubbed fashion cotton; 4.00 mm crochet hook; 0.75 cm × 3 cm (1½ in) metre petersham ribbon (optional).

Tension

10 sts to 5 cm (2 in).

To make

Make 120 ch.

Row 1 Into the third ch from the hook work 1 dc, 1 dc into each ch to end, 1 ch, turn. (119 sts)

Row 2 dc to end, 1 ch, turn. Work a further 10 rows dc. This is the band that will be doubled over the stiffening petersham ribbon. If no stiffener is to be used work only 6 rows in all in dc.

Figure 14 *Two ways in which crochet complements suede: rectangular crochet patches on one and blue suede chevron on the other*

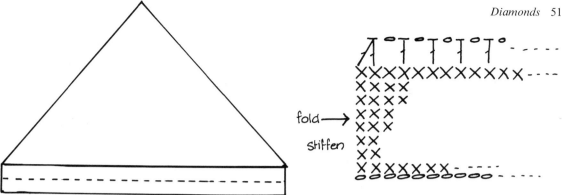

Diagram 42 Head cover

Triangle
Row 1 4 ch, miss 1 st, tr in next st, * 1 ch, miss 1 st, 1 tr in next st, rep from * to last st. (59 sts)

Row 2 4 ch, dec 1 sp (by using next 2 trs and ignoring ch bet), tr 2 tog, * 1 ch, 1 tr in next tr, rep from * to last 3 sps, tr 2 tog, 1 ch, 1) tr in 3rd ch. (57 sts)

Rep row 2 until 3 sts remain.

Final row 3 ch, 3 tr tog (to make a point). Fasten off.

4. Diamonds

A diamond shape is composed of two triangles (whose hypoteneuse is shorter than its two equal sides) joined together at the short side.

Crocheted diamonds can be obtained by:

a Increasing from a point to the width required and then decreasing evenly to match the increases.

b Starting with a foundation chain (as a design detail) across the centre of the diamond to the width needed and then decreasing to a point. Rejoin yarn to foundation chain and repeat the decreasing process.

c Working from the centre as though for a square. One pair of opposite points will have more increases than in a square (i.e. four or five extra stitches), whilst the other two opposite points will have less, (i.e. one or two extra stitches). The combination of four and two extra stitches works quite well.

Points to watch for when working diamonds
1) The four sides should be smooth (see the points to watch for in making triangles on page 49).
2) If using diamonds in another medium such as leather, it may be necessary to round the corners of the material being used so that the tips do not poke through the crochet. The crochet can then use both its increases and stitch heights to produce the point needed.

3) Squares can be used for shorter, squat diamonds. The weight of the work will often elongate the square into an obvious diamond shape.

Items that can be made with diamonds
They are suited to ponchos, settee/sofa covers, table centres, aprons or bags.

The poncho (figure 15) shows the use of one diamond for a garment.

Although the following 'diamond sweater' was based on a diamond shape, in fact two different yarns have been used for each diamond, so it is a debatable point as to whether the sweater is based on triangles or diamonds! The 'luxury' look is obtained by using a different yarn for *every* half diamond.

The black and white photograph (figure 16) seems to show a symmetry of yarns; however this is an illusion as no same two yarns were used for any half diamonds throughout the sweater. Each yarn was an off-white colour which gives a monochromatic effect (page 52), whilst no two are exactly the same shade.

One further point to note: if the overall 'luxury' look is to be achieved, it is necessary to include a variety of fashion yarns that have different textures and different fibre contents.

Diamond sweater (Figure 16)

Size
Adjust diamond for fit.

Materials
26 different yarns of sufficient length to make half a diamond (see note on the yarns above). The hook size should be the largest that the yarn can take without the fabric being too open. Look at figure 16 for guidance.

Figure 15 *This poncho shows an exciting range of stitches and colour*

Figure 16 *Diamond-shapes produce a luxury winter warmer*

To make

First draw to scale a diamond as shown in diagram 43, page 53. The 50 × 25 cm size makes up to a 102 cm (40 in) bust. The 44 × 22 cm size makes up to a 88 cm (34 in) bust. Cut out the diamond in card or very stiff paper. This shape has to be used extensively so flimsy paper will tear. Work in trebles throughout.

Commence at a sharp point of the diamond shape with one yarn. Increase to the centre of the diamond. Change yarn and decrease to the point. It may be necessary to change hook size and alter the number of stitches being used. Do not expect both halves of the same diamond to necessarily be the same either in the

number of rows, the number of stitches, or the look of the fabric.

Make 10 diamonds in all.

Important: It is unwise to use one of the crocheted diamonds as a template. Always use the cardboard shape to measure the work.

Make 5 half diamonds worked in the same direction as the diamond. Work 1 half diamond commencing at the wider point using a very soft and heavily textured yarn. This is the collar. There should be sufficient of this yarn left for the sleeve and hem trim.

Arrange the diamonds as shown in diagram 44 and join along the thick lines with a complementary yarn in

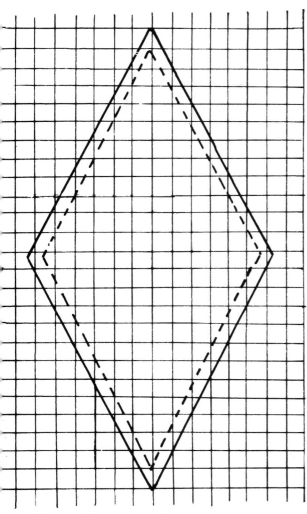

Diagram 43   1 square = 2 cm

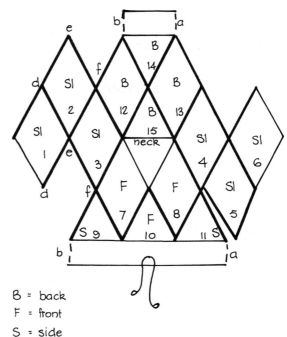

B = back
F = front
S = side
Sl = sleeve

Diagram 44 Assembling diamonds to make a sweater

Crab stitch (i.e. one that blends into the sweater rather than makes the edges of the diamonds more important than the diamonds themselves).

Diamonds 1, 2, 3 fold into each other to form the right sleeve.

Diamonds 4, 5, 6 fold into each other to form the left sleeve.

Diamonds 12 and 13 form the back with triangle 15 fitting into back neck and triangle 14 sitting in the waist.

Diamonds 7 and 8 form the front with triangle 10 sitting in the waist.

Triangles 9 and 11 go underarm and join to a front and a back diamond.

The remaining triangle should have the straight edge attached to the neck sides of diamonds 7 and 8.

Welt

Work 3 or 4 rows treble on the stitches of triangles 9, 10, 11 and 14. Finish with 2 rows dc using the heavily textured yarn.

Sleeve and neck edges

Work 1 row dc using the heavily textured yarn, round back neck edge, and round sleeve ends.

Drawstring

A tie was made of the yarn used to join the diamonds by working a chain using three thicknesses at once. Thread this chain through the first row of trebles made at the welt. Add 2 pom-poms, tassels or balls of dc using the luxury yarn of the edgings.

5. Circles/semi-circles

Circles and semi-circles can be made by:
a Commencing at the middle and increasing by the same number of stitches on each round. For instance if the stitches on round 1 are 6: round 2 = 12,

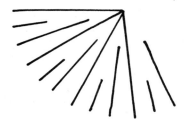

Diagram 45 Sideways working to make a circle (use of stitch heights increases its effectiveness)

Diagram 46 Circles joined to the depressions made by the circles of the previous row produce angles as in a triangle

round 3 = 18, round 4 = 24. A common error in making circles is the inclusion of too many increases per round. NB: It is necessary to stagger the points of increasing to obtain a smooth circle.

b Working in straight rows from centre to circumference. This means working part rows between the full rows. (See diagram 45.)

c Working from the circumference to the centre. This method is more likely to be useful in yokes, or where the centre of the circle is not being filled in.

Points to watch for when making circles/semi-circles

1) The circle frilling instead of lying flat indicates there are too many stitches for the size of the circumference.

Possible ways to correct this:
  (i) have less increases per round;
  (ii) use a larger crochet hook for the pattern;
  (iii) elongate the stitches so that the circumference is further away from the centre of the circle.

2) If the central section of the circle buckles (usually where the pattern changes from a dense close fabric to a lacier pattern to complete the article), check that the chains being made in the lacier section are not too tight. Alternatively use a smaller crochet hook for the central section.

3) The whole circle is bowl-shaped:
  (i) check the stitches are not being accidentally lengthened at the insertion point;
  (ii) check that the chains are not too tight resulting in the circle being pulled in;
  (iii) there could be insufficient increases per round.

4) Semi-circles are extremely difficult to keep straight along the line of the diameter. This is in the way the stitches lie because their natural opposite stitches are missing and there is no opposing pull to make them conform.

5) When placing small circular motifs together it is possible to join them to their neighbour during the last row. However this is only satisfactory if the circles lie within the depressions made by a line of circles (see diagram 46); a good way to reduce into a triangular shape. Should you want to place circular motifs one on top of another in both directions to form a rectangular item, then it is often necessary to crochet 'filler' motifs or alternatively embroider a 'filler' (diagram 47).

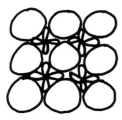

Diagram 47 Filler stitches may be needed if circles are put in rows both horizontally and vertically

Items that can be made with circles and semi-circles
Particularly appropriate are baby shawls, bedjackets, capes, collars, yokes, hats, and myriad household items.

Colourful two-layer beret (Diagram 48, figure 17)

This is a net or post-war snood that has a flat circle of textured colour inserted beneath the net.

Size
Inner circle 23 cm (9 in).

Materials
25 g white mohair for 'snood'; 25 g scraps of vibrant colours of mohair for inner circle. 7.00 mm hook.

To make
This is a flexible pattern. The colour sequence is an individual decision, as is the place to insert a popcorn or cluster.

Figure 17 Vibrant colour adds interest to simple shapes: a beret with colour added underneath to peep through; a bolero has colour added on top for an eye-catching effect

Diagram 48 Brightly-coloured textured circle changed into a beret with crochet net overlay

First layer (*net*) With white mohair and 7.00 mm hook work 4 ch, join with ss. 6 ch * 1 dc in ring, 5 ch, rep from * twice, 3 ch, 1 dtr in ring.

Rnd 2 * 5 ch, 1 dc in next loop, rep from * to end.

Rnd 3 * 5 ch, 1 dc in loop, 5 ch, 1 dc in dc, rep from * to last 2 loops, 5 ch, 1 dc in loop, 3 ch, 1 dtr in dc.

Rnd 4 as rnd 2.

Rnd 5 as rnd 3.

Rnd 6 As rnd 2.

(NB: This should be sufficiently large for an average head. It is here, however, that the pattern can be adjusted by working rnd 3 and 2 once more.)

Rnd 7 3 ch, 1 tr in same place, *2 tr in next loop, rep from * to end, join with ss.

Rnd 8 1 ch, 1 dc in each tr to end, join with ss.

Rnd 9 As rnd 8.

Fasten off.

Inner circle

This is a flat circle of trebles which should remain quite flat with no textured bobbles appearing on the side of the circle that will lie against the head.

Make 4 ch, join with a ss.

Rnd 1 3 ch, 11 tr in ring, join with ss.

Rnd 2 change colour at least twice at irregular intervals on this round, place 1 popcorn (i.e. 6 trebles in the same st, remove hook, draw loop through first tr of 6

just made – 1 popcorn) in each colour change at a point where there is a space between the chain loops of the first layer so that the colour can poke through the net to the right side. 24 sts in all.

Rnd 3 As round 2 but ending with 36 sts.

Rnd 4 As round 2 but ending with 48 sts.

Attach the inner circle using the ends of the scraps of yarn to secure into the backs of the white stitches.

For the use of circular motifs as part of a larger article see Maggi Jo's sweater on page 81.

Many patterns of circular motifs are available, particularly in the cotton 'lace' crochet patterns.

6. Ovals

All the points made for circles apply equally to ovals.

To make ovals to your own design, use a suitable circular motif or traditional round mat pattern and divide it across the diameter. Between these two semi-circles work straight rows of a matching design (see diagram 49).

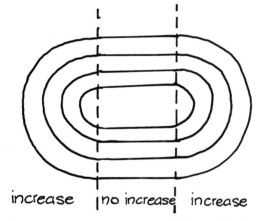

increase | no increase | increase

Diagram 49 Increases for ovals follow principle of circles leaving the central portion without additional stitches

The starting chain is a length of chain worked into twice with the chain at each end being treated as a semi-circle. The number of increases per round are the same as a circle but are confined to each end, i.e. half the increases in one semi-circle and the rest in the other semi-circle.

Items that can be made with ovals

They include ponchos, rugs, blankets, and tablecloths.

7. Other shapes

Symmetrical motifs

Pentagons, hexagons, octagons, etc. are easily worked from the centre, placing the increases in the same positions on each round to form points. As the motif or shape becomes larger, the distance between the points of increase lengthens. What is happening therefore is a series of straight rows connected by increases that form peaks and ultimately connect into a round. To obtain a specific shape, divide the number of increases required to keep a flat circle by the number of points in the shape. This may mean that on one round a point will have two extra stitches but on the next round only one (e.g. an octagon made of trebles, see diagram 50 below).

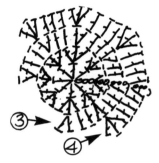

Diagram 50 Increasing an octagon shape in trebles requires rows 3, 5, 7, etc., to have only one extra stitch at each point, while rows 2, 4, 6, etc. need two extra stitches at each point

Joining symmetrical shapes

(i) *To produce a neat tailored finish*

Check that each motif is the same size. It is quite amazing how the state of our physical and emotional well-being can show in the work. If we are controlling pain or are 'on-edge' with emotional stress, then the crochet becomes tighter. Conversely, on holiday without a care in the world and the physical body fully relaxed, the crochet can be looser. In an item that is not made of small regular shapes, the difference in such tensions may pass unnoticed. However, when it comes to placing motifs together, any such personal changes become obvious. This possible variation in size between the motifs may mean that block pressing is necessary. Cotton motifs are in fact better pressed but if it can be avoided with wool and acrylic motifs, then do so.

Block pressing In general, pressing crochet is a much debated subject. Again there are no rigid rules but the following guidelines have been found to work quite well for all yarns with the exception of cotton and linen.

1. Do not press work if surface or raised stitches are incorporated.
2. Be very wary of pressing acrylic with a damp cloth as this causes the yarn to stretch.
3. Only lightly press background fabrics, e.g. double crochets, trebles, etc.

To block press, pin the work onto a blanket starting from the centre of each side or from four quarters of a circle. Have the pinheads nestling into the blanket and not the work. Continue to pin on each side working in opposite pairs. (See diagram 51.)

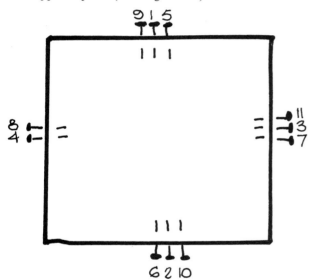

Diagram 51 Insert pins for the preparation of block pressing, in the numerical order as shown

With a damp cloth cover the pinned-out article. Use a hot iron and press over the cloth. Do not move the iron, just press firmly. When all the article has been pressed, remove the cloth and *lightly* iron work. Leave the crochet pinned out until completely dry when it can be removed from the blanket. NB: A cotton cloth is best for pressing.

Now arrange the motifs and design to your personal satisfaction.

Join 1 Sew with a flat unnoticeable stitch such as an over-sew or slip-hem stitch.

Join 2 Double crochet the motifs together on the

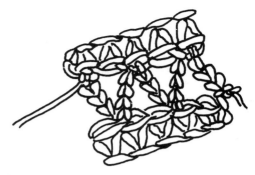

Diagram 52 Linking motifs with small chain loops connected with a slip stitch

wrong side. This produces a ridged effect on one side which may prevent the item being reversable. Unless the last row of each motif is the same colour, avoid this method of joining.

Join 3 Faggot-style join. Link the motifs with small chain loops commencing at the edge of one motif with a slipstitch, then two or three chains and a slip stitch to the opposite motif. Repeat the last two operations to the end. (See diagram 52.)

This gives a neat and reversible join but will produce a larger article than the two joins given above. Allow for this by working one row less on each motif should the size be crucial and the open join more in keeping with the overall effect desired for the item.

(ii) *To produce a textured and/or flamboyant finish*
Idea 1 Crab stitch the motifs together on the right side of the work. The strongest lines are achieved by connecting the motifs in short pieces and then working the long strips together. (See diagram 53.)
(NB: Circles will probably have been joined and can be treated as an octagon.)

Diagram 53 Crab stitch

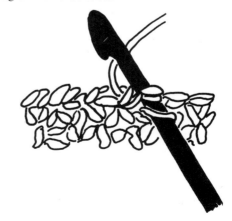

Idea 2 Deliberately work the final row to create fullness. Pinch the fullness evenly to form corresponding 'pleats' to its opposite number *or* create irregular undulations throughout.

Idea 3 Work the final row with irregular spaces and stitch heights. Connect with the Faggot-style *Join 3* above and allow the varied spaces to pull into a 'mock Irish' crochet net join. This can be accentuated if picots are added both to the final row of the motifs and in the connecting chain links.

Idea 4 Work the very centre of the motif in loop stitch (see page 68) using a textured yarn.

Idea 5 For precise neat texture commence the motif with a raised 'rose' pattern. Again the motifs used in Irish crochet are most suitable. Alternatively use the overlapping petal motif that forms the design of the summer top (see page 40). A first row worked over two or three thicknesses of the yarn will add a padded centre to the motif and increase the textured effect.

Idea 6 Use colour to form shapes within the final shape that is additional to the small motifs being used. You can do no better than look to the patchwork quilters for ideas of this nature.

Irregular shapes

They can be controlled to form part of a symmetrical shape by working from the unusual to the usual rather than vice-versa. This is a particularly useful technique when materials other than crochet are being included. (See pages 105–15)

To commence first make any shape, in any stitches and any yarns. Allow it to have curves, straight edges *and* points. At this stage be as uninhibited and unconventional as you wish.

Next, decide what final shape this free form is going to become. Draw to scale the final shape onto a large paper (old parcel paper will do). Now arrange the crochet form on the paper in the position that it will be when completed. The next step is to decide:

(i) whether you are working the controlled and final shape direct from the motif just finished;
(ii) whether you are crocheting from the shape and including the irregular free form when it is reached.

If you are starting to crochet directly onto the free form, start by filling in the deepest indentations (**a**) until there is some levelling off. Any appendages or unsupported offshoots in the free form have been anchored (i.e. controlled). (See example: diagram 54.)

Having anchored the longer, looser and malleable pieces, fill in the shallower indentations (**b**) even to the

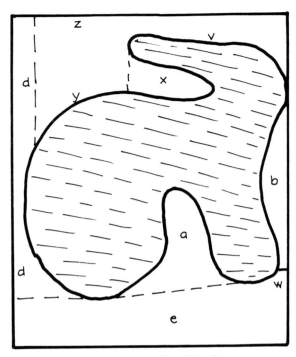

Diagram 54 Building up an irregular shape to a pre-determined outline

point where a false side is manufactured (**w**). Again stop when the levelling-off stage is reached.

The area (**x**) can be treated as (**a**). Alternatively crochet from (**y**) to (**z**). The alternative is possible because of the straight side (**v**).

Crochet (**d**).

Finally crochet (**e**).

Make the suitable edging or join to the larger article of which the regular shape is a part.

Possible difficulties when converting an irregular shape to a regular shape.

1) *Problem* The fill-in rows have holes at the points where they join the motif.

Answer Link the fill-in row carefully. There is no one way to do this but it is important that the last stitch of the fill-in row is part of the irregular motif and the join is not just part of an after-thought. Either work the connecting point of the motif at the same time as the last part of the fill-in stitch is being worked, or remove the hook from the last fill-in stitch and draw it through the motif.

2) *Problem* The fill-in rows pull the sides of the motif in.

Answer Insufficient stitches being used for the filling-in section.

3) *Problem* The filling-in section pushes the motif sides away.

Answer Too many stitches being used for the fill-in.

4) *Problem* Reducing stitches in the fill-in section to allow it to lie flat creates holes.

Answer Use the decrease method and use two or three hook insertions in different places, as if making separate stitches, but instead of completing each stitch – which creates a frilling or over-fullness – draw the stitches together at the top as in a decrease.

5) *Problem* Increasing stitches in the fill-in section creates a lump at the base of the row.

Answer Place the extra stitches in the same place so that only the top of the work has the increase and the base of the stitches are not taking up any more room.

6) *Problem* The rows of the fill-in are not horizontal but are forming ever noticeable diagonals where one side of the motif's fill-in area will be completed before the other.

Answer Use the heights of the various stitches intelligently and to your advantage.

7) *Problem* When extra fill-in areas are completed the original motif has or is changing shape.

Answer Whilst the controlling areas of crochet are being worked there has not been sufficient checking of how the whole is looking. To produce a good finish in this type of work it is important to look at the whole and not at the small area being worked on at that moment. Again it is not possible to take short cuts and be completely pleased with the result. This is one time when crochet *needs* a flat surface on which the final sketch and paper shape is placed. At each stage continuous checks should be made. Only when the whole free form is anchored and straight rows to increase its size are being crocheted can the worker go back to the easy chair and the TV.

The uses of irregular motifs are as limitless as the shapes that can be made.

Section C
Textured crochet

Hunting through the dictionary to ensure the word 'texture' was not misused, it was quite a surprise to find that textile and texture were so closely related to 'text' and the written word. All references to woven material were completely absorbed and staggered throughout the definitions of and references to written communication. As appropriate as this is to someone writing about the subject of fabric, it did make me realise that the much-used word 'texture' has a whole range of inferences that are relatively modern in usage. Because of this and to help you understand what is meant within these pages, *my* definition of 'texture' is 'the tactile nature or feel of a material'. What I mean by 'textured' is 'the inclusion of irregularities within the making of the basic material that changes the smoothness of an almost two-dimensional item into a three-dimensional material'. This latter has been achieved when a strong beam of light creates shadows and highlights within its rays.

A crochet fabric can be created that makes the observer want to put their fingers into it to feel its 'lumps, bumps and knobbles' by:

a using a heavily textured fashion yarn;

b including stitches that create ruggedness in the fabric;

c working on top of a basic and reasonably smooth fabric.

1. Fashion yarns

The international spinners manufacturing yarns for use by individuals have been extremely inventive recently, producing a large range of yarns that are not only varied in colour but in thickness. In addition, many colours are combined in a variety of ways within one yarn. Similarly many thicknesses can be plied to form a single yarn.

For any one person to experiment with the whole range of colours or colour combinations possible – and the textures and texture combinations also possible – is cost prohibitive. Unless there is a lucrative income, plenty of free time, plus a single-mindedness of purpose, choices have to be made. Many of the fashion yarns are expensive and a wrong choice can not only be disappointing but even prevent further experiments and possibly relegate crochet itself to the bottom of the leisure activities for you. A final worry for most people who crochet purely for pleasure in their spare time, is the relatively recent introduction of 'short-term' manufacture. Often a fashion yarn introduced into the market-place will only have a shelf life of two years. This means that the buying on impulse to make something in the future cannot be undertaken lightly. Therefore:

a the yarn has to be used reasonably quickly if there is a doubt as to the quantity;

b extra yarn has to be purchased; *or*

c the crochet worker has to know at the point of buying exactly what can be done if the yarn runs out after it is no longer being sold in the wool shops.

Obviously the producers hope that the second action will be taken; however, after being 'let down' once or twice, even the most compulsive impulse buyer of yarns thinks twice!

There can be no 'rule-of-thumb' with such a vast range of products but from personal experience the following guidelines have been developed. Like everyone else, I have not tried every yarn available, but unlike most my work gives me a greater opportunity to observe and analyse the various effects yarns have on the textile of crochet.

1) Short-space (2–5 cm) multi-coloured yarns give a dappled effect rather like shaking a paintbrush over the whole in several colours.

2) The even-spaced (15–20 cm) random-dyed yarn produces a blocked effect rather like building bricks.

3) The 'long distance' change of colour, usually wound on cones and often in shades of the same hue, gives a rippled effect. Ideally use this yarn for a one-piece garment – even joining a skirt pattern that is normally made in two sections, to work as one – as it is extremely wasteful to find the place in the colour sequence to match up the two pieces. Otherwise the result looks like someone has delved into the scraps and bits box – not even the oddment box – to make the article up! .

4) Soft slubbed yarns: if the yarn is heavily slubbed use quite a large hook and a double crochet stitch. This will increase the 'slubbed look' rather than flatten the yarn.

5) Hard, tight knops in yarn such as cotton and linen threads: again aim towards the larger hook range to allow the knops to be worked with comfort. Too small a hook makes hard work of the crochet, often splitting the bullion-type lumps. One point to watch here is the laundering of such a garment. If it is hung whilst wet the whole article will drop and becomes mis-shapen. However, if it is spun (even washed in a pillowcase) and then laid flat to finish the drying (as long as the garment has been patted into its correct size and shape first) there should be no problems.

6) Bouclé or looped yarns are often unbrushed mohair. Mohair has the properties of combining lightness with warmth. Err on the side of the too large hook to give a luxury effect of softness, rather than lose the loops in the density of a stitch structure.

7) Long haired yarns such as brushed mohairs again have the properties of warmth and lightness, so lean towards the larger hooks. The yarns with a higher proportion of natural fibre, such as the 78% mohairs, can take quite large hooks. The brushed acrylics need to be light-weight when finished but the hook size should be in accordance to the thickness of the yarn rather than increasing the size of the hook too much. As with all fabrics one has to find the balance between lightness of fabric, warmth and practicality. It is quite pointless making something beautiful that will not wash or wear.

8) Thick cord is available, similar to the soft furnishing cords but more colourful and exotic. This is a yarn that is difficult to use on its own but, as part of the design in another material, works quite well. Again use the simplest of stitches and, if it is combined with a fine yarn, crochet over it occasionally to give the illusion of threaded cord rather than crocheted cord.

9) Chenille: as long as this is not too dense, double crochet or trebles give the whole a velvet-type finish. It works well with a smooth yarn between.

10) Shaggy or fringe-type yarns (including chunky bouclé) are usually quite thick. Keep to a simple stitch to allow the effect to be used to its fullest extent (see the Diamond sweater on page 51). This is expensive to buy and a 50 g ball does not go very far. Like all the very unusual yarns, used carefully as a feature in its own right it is delightful to use.

The variety of colour combinations within a textured yarn is limitless. The spinning manufacturers use the simple process of plying two threads together to obtain many of the present fashion yarns. For instance: a cotton bouclé with a rayon knop; space-dyed thin cotton with a single colour knopped cotton; brushed acrylic with a random flexed smooth/brushed thread; two short-spaced bouclé mixed fibre threads to form a rope of loops that look like a packet of dolly-mixture sweets; a cotton, linen or rayon smooth fine thread to 'hold' the looser fibres of softly twisted acrylics and wools.

Ribbon yarns can be purchased with a matt or a shiny finish; single or multi-coloured; with a loop fringe edge, or flat. Some have picots along one side. Treat these as any luxury yarn and aim to enhance the beauty of their construction rather than flatten it in a dense fabric or complicated stitch structure.

One point worth noting is that the crochet hook handles the most complicated yarn very well, particularly if the hook chosen is not too small. It produces a dense looking fabric but is in fact lightweight to wear, usually using less yarn than its knitted counterpart. The jacket which follows is a good example of this.

If the yarn being used is heavily textured, rugged in different ways and colourful, then the only thing to do is let the yarn do the designing for you. Keep the shape of the finished article relatively uncluttered with as few design lines as possible. At the same time keep the stitch structure basic. Often even a treble stitch will reduce the beauty of the yarn as it appears in the ball.

A tip to help make up your mind how to use the yarn is to observe how the yarn was being displayed for sale, particularly at exhibitions. If it was pushed together in balls in a confined area, double crochet and simplicity will work. If it is on hanks to display the length of colour or distance between the slubs/knops etc., know that the way the colour falls in the garment can create problems unless it is analysed first. Beautiful yarns in hanks need a little more thought in planning how to use it. The final item should be as tempting as the hank.

One final tip when using heavily textured fashion yarns: face the window and have the light in front of you, not behind as with other crafts. The light will shine through the holes in the fabric and the place to insert the hook for the next stitch will become more obvious.

Dolly Mixture jacket
(Diagram 55, figure 18, colour plate 8)

One size only
85 cm (approx. 34 in). Back length: 58 cm (23 in).

Materials
12 balls Welcomme 'La De Dion Bouton' bouclé; 3 balls Welcomme 'Le Maxi-Mohair' of a complementary colour.
Size 12.00 mm and 10.00 mm crochet hooks.

Tension
WORK LOOSELY or the effect of the yarn is spoilt.
3 sts to 5 cm (2 in).

This pattern starts with a centre back panel worked from hem to neck, continued over the shoulders and down the front. From this the central sleeve panel is worked. The sleeve and side panels are then worked. Finally the front and neck border is added.

To make
With the bouclé yarn and 12.00 mm hook make 21 ch. Work loosely! (If necessary try a 15.00 mm hook.)
Row 1 1 dc in 3rd ch from hook, 1 dc in each ch to end, 1 ch turn.
Row 2 dc to end, 1 ch turn.
Continue in dc until 33 rows have been completed.

Diagram 55 Working directions and final shape of jacket made from heavily textured yarn

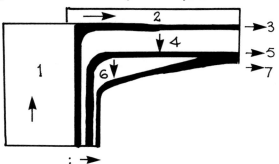

Divide for shoulder and fronts
* Work 5 rows on first 5 sts, 4 ch.
Next row 1 dc in 3rd ch from hook, dc to end.
Work 29 rows on these 8 sts.
Fasten off. **
As this yarn is so heavily textured it is possible to rejoin the bouclé yarn into the beginning of the back piece.
Work from * to ** for other front.
Rejoin yarn to 31 st row on straight edge, 1 ch, 1 dc in each of next 6 row ends. (30 rows remain.)
Work a further 29 rows of dc on these 7 sts. Fasten off.
Work other sleeve panel to match.
Choose a right side. With RS facing join maxi-mohair to base of back.
1 ch. Work 1 dc in each row end of side of back and down sleeve, 1 ch turn. Work 1 row dc back along these stitches.(NB: It may be necessary to put 2 dc at curve, for movement.)
With RS facing for all first rows, repeat the pattern of 2 rows dc to balance front of sleeve.
Do other sides to match.
With bouclé yarn and RS facing, join to base of back centre panel in the mohair.
1 ch, dc up back and down sleeve, 1 ch turn.
Next row dc to corner, link with ss 1 ch, underarm turn.
Next row dc to end, 1 ch, turn.
Repeat these 2 rows once and fasten off.
Work the other 3 sides to match.
With maxi-mohair, work 2 rows dc up side of body and down sleeve. Fasten off.
Join bouclé yarn to underarm corner, 1 ch, 21 dc, turn.
Next row ss over 7 sts, dc to end, 1 ch turn.
Next row 13 dc, turn.
Next row ss over 3 sts, dc to end, 1 ch turn.
Next row 5 dc, fasten off.
Work 3 other wedge-shaped panels to correspond.
With maxi-mohair, work 1 row dc up side and along sleeve, 1 ch turn.
Next row dc to underarm.
One of the 4 sides will correspond to this instruction. The other 2 sides will need to have the yarn joined in from underarm.
Join underarm and side seams in one.

Front and neck border
Row 1 With RS facing and maxi-mohair join yarn to base of right front. Work 1 dc in each row end up front, over shoulder, across back neck, over shoulder and down front, 1 ch turn.
Row 2 dc to corner, 2 dc in corner st at front neck, dc to inner front neck corner, dc 2 tog over front neck and

Figure 18 *Styled with fashion yarns (colour close-up, plate no. 8)*

Plate 1 Kathleen Basford's 'Marine Life', inspired by David Bellamy's 'Botanic Man', reproduces corals and sea anemones, etc.

Plate 2 Use of thrums to create a simple top that gives the illusion of a suburban garden as seen through tear-filled eyes

Plate 3 Joan Hadwin's 'Flower Power', a controlled use of vivid colours

Plate 4 Surface crochet in two panels of open-weave mohair with the panels being connected by textured yarn

Plate 5 Simple collage allowing the yarn to do the work

Plate 6 Blocks of colour worked from a chart so that only one yarn is used at any one time

Plate 7 Co-operative collage made by students on a course at a summer school in Morecambe: an example of random colour use

Plate 8 Close up of the mixed colours and textures contained in a commercially produced fashion yarn (see figure 17 for jacket style)

Plate 9 Surface crochet added to a knitted sleeve to make an already luxurious coat exclusive

Plate 10 Mary Cheadle's 'TreeBeard'

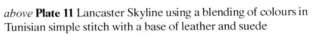

above **Plate 11** Lancaster Skyline using a blending of colours in Tunisian simple stitch with a base of leather and suede

left **Plate 12** Crocheted fuse wire for impact

Plate 13 Fungi collage

shoulder, dc over shoulder, dc 2 tog at shoulder and back neck, dc across back neck, dc 2 tog at back neck and shoulder, dc over shoulder, dc 2 tog at shoulder and front neck, 2 dc in corner, dc to end. Fasten off.
Row 3 Join in bouclé, work 1 row dc. Fasten off.
Row 4 With RS facing, join in maxi-mohair to base of right front, dc to end.
Row 5 With RS still facing change to 10.00 mm hook. Work 1 row Crab stitch. Fasten off.

Chevron overtop (Diagram 56, figure 19)

This pattern is for those who are familiar with the chevron pattern principle.

One size only
91 cm (36 in) bust. Back length 63 cm (25 in).

Materials
400 g pure wool very chunky heavy bouclé wool such as Dilthey Loope Wolle; 100 g DK bouclé such as Calvados in a contrast.
10.00 mm hook.

Tension
1 chevron patt = 10 cm (4 in) wide.
3 row rep = 9 cm (3½ in) deep.

To make in the round
Rnd 1 Make 62 ch, 2 tr in 4th ch from hook. * 1 tr in next ch, tr 3 tog, 1 tr in next ch, 3 tr in next ch, rep from * to last 5 ch, 1 tr, tr 3 tog, 1 tr, join with ss. (NB: It is easier to join the chain after to prevent twisting.) (60 sts)
Rnd 2 3 ch turn, 2 tr in same place. * 1 tr, tr 3 tog, 1 tr, 3 tr in next st (centre of 3 tr gr), rep from * to last 5 sts, 1 tr, tr 3 tog, 1 tr, join with ss.
Rnd 3 Change to thin contrast. Using 2 balls together work as rnd 2.
Rnd 4 As rnd 2 in Loope Wolle.
Rnd 5 As rnd 2.
Repeat rounds 3–5 inclusive, twice.

Divide for back
Keep chevron pattern and colour changes.
Work 8 rows keeping edges straight as described on page 41, using 21 sts.
Miss 7 sts under arm and work first front on 12 sts for 9 rows.
Decrease at neck edge by 5 sts leaving 7 sts for shoulder join.
Miss 1 st and work second front on next 12 sts reversing the shapings.
Join shoulder seams.

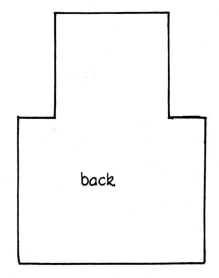

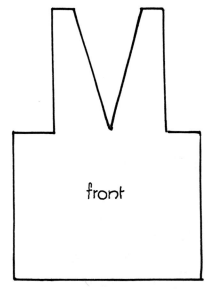

Diagram 56 Chevron overtop in a thick textured fashion yarn

To complete
Work 1 row dc to neck.
Work 1 row dc at each armhole.
NB: Watch the borders do not frill.
There is no need to add a finishing row to the hem.

Figure 19 *Pure wool bouclé gives the effect of a sheep's fleece*

2. Stitches to create a rugged texture

Much of this has been covered in the sections on textured trebles (page 28) and long trebles (page 32).

The use of different stitch heights, as shown in the bouclé stitch in the sleeveless unisex sweater (page 33), created a bobbled unevenness to the fabric. In that instance the difference in height between the two stitches was sufficient to push the treble stitch downwards, particularly as there was a row of basic standard size stitches following. The sleeveless sweater below, however, uses the stitch heights to create a more gentle but nonetheless interesting texture. This has been described as pebble, crazy and sand stitch in different patterns over the past 50 years. The longer stitch (i.e. the treble) leans over the shorter stitch (i.e. the double crochet) to find its level. On the way back, as the crochet fabric is turned on each row, the treble is worked into the double crochet and the double crochet in the treble, thus balancing up the leaning. If this stitch is worked in an unsmooth yarn it may sometimes be difficult to find which stitch should be worked next.

Sleeveless sweater (Diagram 57)

Size

76(86/96/106) cm; 30(34/38/42) in.
Back length: approx. 135 cm (26 in)

Materials

400 g (450 g/550 g/600 g) washable Aran.
6.00 mm and 7.00 mm crochet hooks.

Tension

Over crazy stitch pattern worked on 7.00 mm hook: 5 sts to 5 cm (2 in), 6 rows to 5 cm (2 in).
Make sure the tension is correct before working as it is easy to work too tightly when using larger hooks for the first time.

To make
Back

Using 7.00 mm crochet hook make 44(50/54/60) ch loosely.
Row 1 1 dc in 4th ch from hook, *1 tr in next ch, 1 dc in next ch, rep from * to end, 3 ch turn. (42[48/52/58] sts)
Row 2 * 1 dc on next st (which should be a tr), 1 tr on next st (which should be a dc), rep from * to last st, 1 dc in last st, 3 ch, turn.
Repeat row 2, 31 times (approx. 28 cm), omit turning ch on last row.
Row 34 ss across 6(6/8/8) ch, 3 ch, 1 dc, * 1 tr, 1 dc, rep from * leaving the last 6(6/8/8) sts unworked, 3 ch, turn. 30(36/36/42) sts **
Repeat row 2, 29 times. Break off yarn.

Front

Work as back to **. Repeat row 2, 26 times.
Next row 1 dc, * 1 tr, 1 dc, repeat from * 2(3/3/4) times, 3 ch turn. (8[10/10/12] sts)
Work row 2, 7 times. Break off yarn.
Join yarn into neck for second shoulder by missing 14(16/16/18) sts, 3 ch, 1 dc, * 1 tr, 1 dc, rep from * to end, 3 ch, turn. Repeat row 2, 7 times.
Join shoulder seams.
Join side seams.

Welt

Using 6.00 mm hook join yarn to a side seam, 3 ch, 1 tr in each st along front and back. (84[96/102/116] sts)
Work the next 5 rows in raised treble rib. (See page 29.)

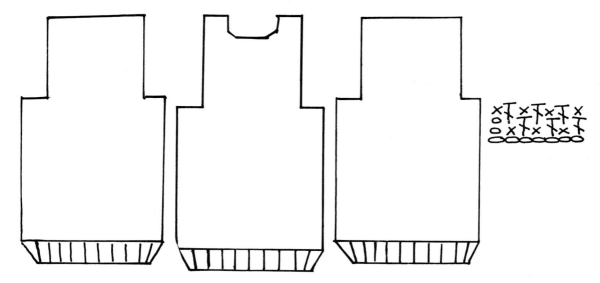

Diagram 57 Sleeveless sweater

Armhole borders

With 6.00 mm hook join yarn to underarm seam, 2 ch, 1 tr in each stitch to corner, put 2 sts in corners carefully to avoid holes. (It is possible to cheat in crochet and this may be a good time to try.) Put 15 trebles evenly (1 tr every 2 rows) up back and 21 tr over shoulder and down front with 1 tr in each stitch to turning ch, join with a ss, 2 ch, TURN. This is important.

Work 3 rows raised treble rib as for welt, joining with a ss but making sure the work is turned on every row.

Neck border

With 6.00 mm hook join yarn to centre back neck, 2 ch. Place 1 tr in each st to corner, 6 tr evenly over shoulder (watch corner for holes), 14(16/16/18) tr along front, 6 tr over shoulder, 1 tr in each st to centre back. Join with ss, 2 ch turn. Work 3 rows in raised treble rib on these stitches turning on every row. Break off yarn.

A double crochet fabric is an excellent way to include loops to give a shaggy fringed effect. This pattern uses a smooth cotton for a long-lasting bathroom set.

Bathroom set (Diagram 58)

Materials

Quantities depend upon the size of the various covers but, as a guide, approximately 650 g of smooth soft 4- ply cotton (or even a 3-ply) will be needed for the 3 items.

4.50 mm crochet hook.

Sufficient elastic for outer and inner edge.

1 m (1 yd) narrow tape together in dc.

Tension

Tension of all crochet should be 16 rows to 8 cm (3 in) and 4 sts to 2.5 cm (1 in) using *two balls of yarn together* in dc.

Toilet lid

A stiff paper pattern to place the crochet on is a help. Make 10 ch with 2 balls of cotton and 4.50 mm hook.

Row 1 1 dc in 3rd ch from hook, 1 dc in each ch to end, 1 ch turn. (9 sts)

Row 2 Work 1 loop st into each of the dc of previous

Diagram 58 Bathroom set using loop stitch

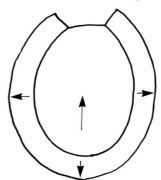

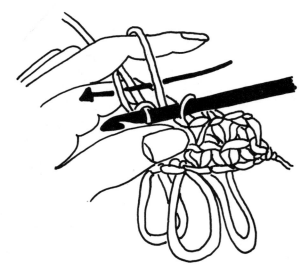

Diagram 59 Loop stitch: the arrow shows direction of hook insertion at next stage of completing the stitch

row by inserting the crochet hook into the top of the first stitch and wrapping yarn round first finger of the left hand. Now put the yarn round the hook, and draw through one stitch. Yarn over hook, draw through 2 sts, then work 1 ch *tightly* to lock the loop into place. This ch is part of the loop stitch and *does not* count as a separate st. 1 ch, turn. (Diagram 59.)

Row 3 1 dc in same place as turning ch, 1 dc in each loop st, 2 dc in last st. (2 increases made.)

Row 4 Increase at the beginning and end of the row and work in loop st.

Repeat rows 3 and 4 until there are 51 sts or until the crochet fits the top of the lid exactly.

Work approximately 40 rows for the main part of the lid, which should take you to the end of the widest part.

Decrease 1 st at each end of next 13 rows leaving 25 sts still to work. This should bring the crochet to the hinged part of the lid.

Leave the central 11 sts (or whatever number is required for your hinge) and work 1 dc into the first 6 sts (7 sts with turning ch), 1 ch, turn.

Work 1 row of dc all round seat top using approximately 7 dc over hinge piece, 1 dc in the end of every other decrease row, 1 dc in each of the straight row ends, 1 dc in the end of every alternate increase row, 1 dc in each of the turning ch, 1 dc in alternate increase rows, 1 dc in each straight row, 1 dc in alternate decrease rows, 7 dc, 1 ch, turn.

Next row 1 row dc using 1 dc for each dc of last row, 1 ch, turn. (Unless the lid is a very thick one of the older variety, 1 row dc to take the crochet over the edge is sufficient.)

Next row *(decrease 1 dc over 2 sts) 4 times, 1 dc, repeat from * to end, 1 ch, turn.

Last row 1 row dc. Make 40 ch for a tie, fasten off and darn in ends.

Rejoin yarn to other side of hinge, make 40 ch, and fasten off.

Toilet seat cover

This is a suitable accessory for people with brittle bone or circulatory problems. Ideally two should be made as one will frequently be in the wash. Make 21 ch, (still with two balls of yarn together and a 4.50 mm crochet hook).

Row 1 1 dc in 3rd ch from hook, 1 dc in each ch to end, 2 ch, turn. (20 sts)

Row 2 miss 1 st, 1 dc in next and every stitch to the last 2 sts, 1 ch, miss 1 st, 1 dc in last st, 1 ch, turn.

Row 3 1 dc in 1 ch sp, 1 dc in each dc to end, 1 dc in 1 ch sp, 1 dc in turning ch, 2 ch turn.

Row 4 as row 2.

Row 5 as row 3.

Row 6 as row 2.

Row 7 1 dc in 1 ch sp, 6 dc, 6 htr, 4 tr, 1 tr in 1 ch sp, 1 tr in end.

Repeat rows 2–7 inclusive until sufficient length has been made to cover the seat. Join seam and place near hinge.

Thread elastic through the holes on the inside edge of the seat making sure the crochet curls under the lid lip. Thread tape from the hinge side, leaving approx. 5 holes without tape at the hinge. Have sufficient length to tie.

Pedestal mat

There is no standard size of pedestal for the base of lavatories. Therefore use stiff paper and draw a pattern. Work with 1 row loop stitch and 1 row dc to the size of your paper pattern and finish with 2 rows dc round the edges. Thin foam rubber can be stitched to the back to make it non-slip.

Another way to make a loop stitch is to crochet lengths of chain between the double crochet stitches. This takes up more yarn than the method above but is sometimes essential if a looped effect is needed for the design and the yarn is one that breaks easily. To be able to use the soft yarn and get the loop effect it will be necessary to make chains.

Not only has crochet got a limitless font of stitches and ways in which it can combine with other materials for an endless supply of creative art forms and fashion garments, but it also seems to have a way (as with many other crafts) of crossing international barriers. For instance, reported in a newspaper was the story of the lady found crocheting after a plane crash in a jungle waiting to be rescued.

The Polish Star stitch came into my life by a particularly roundabout route. Mary Davies runs an Esperanto Centre in Heysham and has travelled extensively with her interest. One such trip took her to Poland. Mary speaks no Polish and the people she stayed with spoke no English so all communication was by Esperanto. Besides not speaking Polish, Mary did not crochet(!). However, with a little helpful sign language, when the Esperanto vocabulary was not quite adequate, she mastered the art of the stitch pattern below to make cushions. What is perhaps more surprising is the fact that Mary still insists she cannot crochet as she can only do that one pattern and at the time of talking to me had only made cushion covers!

The effect of this textured stitch is an illusion of quilting. The pattern has been limited to the two front panels in the jacket below to allow the extended treble basic stitch to form a contrast, thus framing the pattern. (See figure 20 for a close up of the stitch.)

Polish Star stitch jacket (Diagram 60)

Size
To fit up to 91 cm (36 in).
Back length 60 cm (23½ in).

Materials
10×50 g acrylic and wool DK in the main colour;
3×50 g acrylic and wool in contrast.
5.00 mm and 4.50 mm hooks.
7 buttons.

Tension
6 sts to 4 cm (1½ in) worked in ordinary trebles with the 4.50 mm hook.

Special pattern stitches
Extended treble (Etr)
Commence to work an extended treble as though working an ordinary treble. There is an additional operation at the beginning of the stitch as follows: yoh, insert hook under 2 strands of next st, yoh, pull through to front (3 loops on hook), yoh, pull through 1 loop (still 3 loops on hook), (yoh, pull through 2 loops) twice – an extended treble made.

⟶ *Direction of work* ⟶

Figure 20 *Polish star stitch*

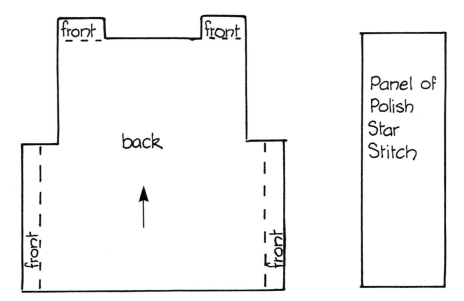

Diagram 60 Jacket incorporating Polish star stitch

Polish Star stitch

This is based on a multiple of 8 sts using an extended treble as given above. The 10 chain loops between the groups of stitches are interlocked before the final row is worked. 2 tones or 2 colours give the best effect. Try a sample piece as follows using two colours of DK and a 5.00 mm hook:

With colour A make 36 ch.

Row 1 In A: 1 Etr in 4th ch from hook, 10 ch, *miss 1 ch, 1 Etr in next 4 ch, 10 ch, miss 1 ch, (2 Etr in next ch) twice, 10 ch, rep from * twice, 4 Etr, 10 ch, miss 1 ch, 2 Etr in last ch. Do not count 10 chains as stitches.

Row 2 In B: 3 ch, turn, 2 Etr in next st, 10 ch, * miss 1 st, 2 Etr, 10 ch, miss 1 st, 2 Etr in next st, 2 Etr, 2 Etr in next st, 10 ch, rep from * twice, miss 1 st, 2 Etr, 10 ch, miss 1 st, 2 Etr in next st, 1 Etr in turning ch. DO NOT TURN WORK.

Row 3 In A: 3 ch to turn on top of turning ch of row 2, 1 Etr, 10 ch, *miss 1 st, (2 Etr in next st) twice, 10 ch, miss 1 st, 4 Etr, 10 ch, rep from * twice, miss 1 st (2 Etr in next st) twice, 10 ch, miss 1 st, 2 Etr.

Row 4 In B: 13 ch, miss 1 st, * 2 Etr in next st, 2 Etr, 2 Etr in next st, 10 ch, miss 1 st, 2 Etr, 10 ch, miss 1 st, rep from * twice, 2 Etr in next st, 2 Etr, 2 Etr in next st, 10 ch, 1 Etr in last st. DO NOT TURN WORK.

Row 5 In A: 3 ch on top of turning ch, 1 Etr in same place, 10 ch, *miss 1 st, 4 Etr, 10 ch, miss 1 st, (2 Etr in next st) twice, 10 ch, rep from * twice, miss 1 st, 4 Etr, 10 ch, miss 1 st, 2 Etr in last st. Rows 2–5 incl. form the basic pattern.

When work is long enough work a final row with A, after the loops have been interlinked (see diagram 60). Interlink stages:

1) Thread RH loop through LH loop where loops are closest. These crossed loops will lie over colour stripe B.
2) Thread colour B through loop A using the nearest B loop lying on the same diagonal line as stage 1.
3) Thread colour A through B keeping the diagonal line.
4) Cross colour A by threading the RH side through the LH side.
   Repeat stages 2–4 inclusive to top of crochet.

Diagram 61 The chains worked between the trebles of the Polish star stitch need to be linked as shown, so that the loose crochet fabric closes in to a regular textile weight and design

Final row In A: work 4 Etr in centre 4 of the 6 Etr in previous row.
Work 1 dc in 10 ch loop. Work 4 Etr in 2 Etr in previous row.
To widen, repeat pattern more times.

Jacket

Back

In A and 4.50 mm hook make 86 ch.
Row 1 1 tr in 4th ch from hook, 1 tr in each ch to end, 3 ch turn. (84 sts)
Row 2 tr to end, 3 ch turn.
Repeat row 2, 23 times – approx. 32 cm (12½ in).

Divide for back

ss over 12 sts, 3 ch, 1 tr in next 59 sts, (leaving 12 sts unworked), 3 ch, turn. (60 sts)
Work a further 18 rows in tr.

Shoulder pieces

Work 5 rows tr on first 15 sts. Fasten off.
Miss 30 sts. Rejoin yarn to next st and work 5 rows tr on the last 15 sts.
Fasten off.

Polish Star stitch fronts (2 alike)

With 5.00 mm hook and M make 44 ch. Follow the pattern as given until work measures approx. 56 cm (22 in). Finish with the final row in M after working a B row.
Join underarm side seam to front panel.
Join shoulder piece to top of front panel.

Sleeves

In A yarn and 4.50 mm hook make 82 ch.
Row 1 1 tr in 4th ch from hook, 1 tr in each ch to end, 3 ch, turn. (80 sts)
Row 2 tr to end, 3 ch turn.
Work 3 further rows tr on these 80 sts.

Row 6 tr 2 tog, tr to end, 3 ch, turn.
Repeat row 6, 33 times.
Row 40 dc to end, 1 ch turn.
Repeat row 40, 4 times.
With RS facing work 1 row Crab stitch. Fasten off.
Join in sleeves.

Neck border

Work 6 rows dc round front necks, shoulders and back neck. (NB: It is not necessary to decrease on these rows as it is a stand up collar. CHECK on the first row that the correct number of stitches have been made and that there is not a hole at any of the corners – particularly front neck to shoulder piece and shoulder piece to back neck.)

Welt

With RS facing and using every stitch, work 1 row dc in A.
Work 5 more rows in dc. Fasten off.

Left-hand front border

With RS facing work 1 row dc. This must be flat! (NB: It may be necessary to work 2 htr occasionally if the 'quilting' has left an uneven edge.) Work a further 5 rows dc. Fasten off.

Right-hand front border

Match *exactly* the number of stitches in this border to that of the left-hand border. Work 2 rows dc.
Buttonhole row Mark the position of the buttons remembering that one button should lie at the neck area and one in the welt. Work this row in dc until a marker is reached. *1 ch at marker, miss 1 st, dc to next marker. Rep to end.
Work a further 2 rows dc.
With RS facing work 1 row Crab stitch all round neck, fronts and welt.
Fasten off. Sew on buttons.

Section D
Use of colour

For longer than I wish to remember I believed that the ability to use colour was a gift you were born with and as I had not been born with this gift, the use of colour would have to remain forever outside the scope of my achievements. So convinced was I that this was a truth that it never entered my head to try to use colour until those fateful days when certain examination papers in my late 20s/early 30s demanded that some basic rudiments of colour were at least thought about. Even then any success was thought of by me as a fluke, good luck, or coincidence – *never* to the fact that it was possible to learn and understand some of its principles and then use them accordingly.

It does not matter at what age one begins to look at colour, there is (as with all learning) a hesitant exploring and practising before colour use becomes instinctive and habitual. It is this unerring instinct of artists that gives rise to the myth that colour concept is born into a person and not an achievement. Of course some people will gain the skills quicker than others but this applies to any form of learning.

The only tools needed are:

a the desire to want to use colour

b a freedom of thought that is not confined to rules of '*always/never/must*' etc. These words largely contribute to holding back a would-be colour user, as they inhibit experimentation.

According to the Lovibond Tintometre, there are 9,000,000 individual colours, so any experimentation is a success, particularly if it is analysed and the results noted and then incorporated in the future. If something has not worked the knowledge that it has not worked is useful. If it *has* worked then that is a bonus not necessarily looked for.

As with all learning of new skills there are guide lines that help the understanding of the ideas behind the thinking. This section follows a logical progression of experimentation with the use of colour. It uses the shapes of the previous section but adds colour in a variety of ways. If this seems to be something you would rather not do, but would still like to make the items given in this section, then simply use multi-coloured or single-coloured yarns as a substitute. The shops today are an Alladin's cave of textured, colourful, mixed-fibre threads, so if you do not wish to mix your own 'paint box' of yarns, let the commercial manufacturers do it for you. However, there does come a time when the interested crochet worker wants the stitch pattern to be the most important part of the article being made. As stated previously, using the colourful commercial yarns usually means keeping to the basic and plainer stitches.

1. Monochromatic

This is the use of all the tones of a single colour. The original hue has either been darkened with varying degrees of black, or lightened with varying degrees of white. It is a simpler way of looking at the effects of highlighting or using undertones in an article, as the experimenter is not being confused with other factors in the colour spectrum. One of the main advantages of working with the various tones of a single colour is that it will be acceptable whatever happens, even if it has not quite made 'First class' in an art award!

Points to remember when working with a single hue are:

a The lightest tone is best used discriminately as a highlight, to add spark or lift. If the item seems 'flat' and monotonous when completed, a small amount of a lighter tone can be applied afterwards either by surface crochet (see Section E) or by embroidery.

b It may be that the overall effect is too bright and the opposite of **a** is needed. A small amount of the darkest tone will give depth and reduce the 'dazzle' of the lighter tones.

c In a garment, bands of different tones can create the illusion of width, height, etc.

d It is possible a ratio will emerge when using bands of different tones. For instance, if five tones are being used to form a shaded skirt which starts at the waist with the lightest tone, the next deeper tone will probably need to use twice as many rows as the first; the next one three times as many rows as the first, the following shade four times, whilst the darkest will probably need to use five times as many rows as the first and lightest tone. This ratio creates a balance (sometimes referred to as weighting a colour). If the skirt was crocheted with the lightest tone having the widest band it would be acceptable but something would appear to be not *quite* right. This is because the weighting would be out of balance. Keeping the same ratio but reversing the colour sequence so that the lightest tone is at the base of the skirt would help a little, but, when compared with the first sequence, even that would only seem *nearly* right. It is rather like seeing a picture that has been taken of houses as reflected in a still lake: if the actual houses are not shown in the picture as well, there is an overwhelming urge to either turn the picture or yourself upside down!

A quick glance through this book shows a number of designs using just two or three colours. Use the technique of using many shades of one colour in these designs by following the tones through the yarn changes. Not only will the exercise stimulate the newcomer to colour usage to become observant of the way the shades relate one to the other but will result in an exclusive garment of your own, as the chances of any two people using the same colour sequence in the same yarns is very remote.

Colour plate 1 is an excellent example of Kathleen Basford's intelligent observation of natural phenomena reproduced in soft shades of grey, which have picked up the hint of blue and green as through a mist. The overall effect is the gentlest blue grey. Much surface crochet is included, each piece carefully selected to fit beautifully into the whole.

For the apprehensive crocheter the following crochet top was in deep wine, with the textured 'bee stitch' in a medium tone of the same hue, and the sunken double crochet row in the lightest of shades of the same hue.

'4-ply for comfort' (Diagram 62, figure 21)

The pattern for the skirt in figure 2 is in Chapter IX on 'Shaping' in *Creative Design in Crochet*.

Size
To fit bust 88–95 cm (34½–37½ in).
Back length incl. knitting: 58 cm (23 in).
Sleeve and yoke stripe section before cuffs measures 117 cm (46 in).

Materials
300 g Forsell 4-ply pure wool; 25 g each of contrast B and C.
4.50 mm hook.
1 pair size 10 knitting needles.

Tension
8 sts to 5 cm (2 in); 4 rows to 9 cm (3½ in).

Abbreviations
M = main colour; B = contrast for textured row; C = contrast for dc row.

To make (2 pieces alike)
This garment is worked from the neck down to the waist so the strip should measure 117 cm (46 in).
Using the 4.50 mm hook make 213 ch in M.
Row 1 1 tr in 4th ch from hook, 1 tr in each ch to end, 3 ch turn. (211 sts)
Row 2 tr to end. Do not break off this yarn.
Row 3 Join in B to the first stitch of row 1 (that is the turning chain before the first treble), 1 tr, 1 ss in next st, * 1 tr, 1 ss in next st, rep from * to end.
Break off yarn. Turn work.
Row 4 Insert hook into the last ss made in B and draw M through, 3 ch, * 1 tr in each st to end. 3 ch, turn.
Row 5 As row 2.
Do not turn work but join in C to the beginning of row 5.
Row 6 1 ch, dc to end. Break off C.
Row 7 Insert hook into the dc just made and draw M through, 3 ch, 1 tr in each st to end. 3 ch turn.
Repeat rows 2–7, 3 times.
Row 26 ss over 24 sts, 2 dc, 2 htr, 156 tr, 2 htr, 2 dc, 1 ss (leaving 23 sts unworked).
Continue only in M from now, turning work on each row as in other patterns.
Row 27 ss over 6, 1 dc, 1 htr, tr to last 8 sts, 1 htr, 1 dc, 1 ss.
Repeat row 27, 6 times. (79 sts)
Work 16 rows in treble on these 79 sts. Break off yarn.
Work another piece exactly the same.
There is a different look to one side of the yoke than

Figure 21 *Complementing a favourite skirt, a 4-ply*
pure wool top that is very comfortable to wear

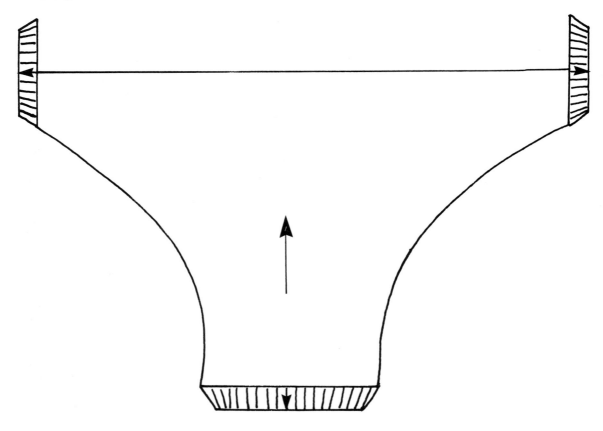

Diagram 62 Easy-to-wear sweater using colour across the shoulders and down the sleeves

the other. The more textured side is the right side. With right sides together join the tops of the sleeves and shoulders by double crocheting the two pieces together for 84 sts on each side, leaving 43 sts unworked for the neck opening. Join underarm and sleeve seams in one. You may find that a *loose* oversewing stitch will be best for this.

Neck
In M work 1 row Crab stitch round the neck opening (see page 57).

Knitted cuffs
Pick up 48 sts along cuff edge. Work 20 rows in knit 1, purl 1 rib. Cast off very loosely.

Knitted welt
Pick up 144 sts. Work 24 rows knit 1, purl 1 rib. Cast off loosely (using the increase method as it is the hip). NB: If the welt needs to be bigger add extra stitches on the first row of the rib.

2. Limited use of the colour wheel

Any art shop should be able to sell you a colour wheel which can be used as an aid to colour selection. Take any small segment of the bought colour wheel and mix together in a pattern the variety of tones that lie within that segment and it is very unlikely that you would be disappointed with the result. However, even with the highlights and the undertones included in the article it may be that you feel there is still something missing. In that case choose a *very* small amount of one of the colour tones that lie exactly opposite the segment used on the colour wheel as a contrast.

Obviously this is not a book on colour and some of the best ways to really learn about colour is:

a to experiment;

b to look at everything around you noting the different tones that are contained in them;

c to borrow or buy books that explain what colour is or simply use colour extensively, i.e. books on travel or nature.

Dress (Figure 22)

The dress pattern uses exactly this technique of limiting one's use of the colour wheel. The 'quiet' period (see page 78) is the off-white shaped and tailored body pieces which contain darts for the waist and for the bust. (See 'Shaping', page 42.)

The apparent random use of colour stripes is based on four shades selected from the pink-to-blue segment of the colour wheel. Just one shade of light green was included. Added to these five colours was the original cream of the body piece, and four neutral tones that linked with this cream.

3. Random use of colour

The opposite to the use of monochromatic and controlled limited use of a single hue is a complete random choice. To create a totally haphazard use of colour make a pile of the oddments of yarn you have around that do not look too awful together. If there is an odd ball in the heap that really makes you feel bilious then remove it, otherwise be adventurous and use the lot. Often that odd ball fits in perfectly anyway! The haphazard selection of colour can be taken to extremes by putting the oddments in a black opaque container and only popping the hand in to select the next colour whilst the eyes are averted, then having the courage to continue with that colour, even if it would not normally have been the one chosen in a freely selective way.

Having gone through this practical experiment once, it is great fun to use it again adding the minimum of control to the yarns selected. It does seem that for most people the very act of having the courage to use the selected yarns without looking, helps the mind to be receptive to colour combinations that are not part of conditioned family and society thinking. Figure 23 on page 79 shows how the plain bands of fabric and the light border and hub, make the semi-circular stained

glass window effect work. This window was the result of a group of 23 people working to numbered cardboard shapes as part of a weeks course work at a Crochet Summer School. The group members had no idea where their pieces went. No-one but myself had made the jigsaw of cardboard pieces nor had anyone else the key. Colour and stitch pattern was left completely to the individual. Thus the whole project was entirely random with minimal control. It was not until the pieces were finally sewn onto the black background on the last morning, that anyone had any idea of where their pieces went or how the end result would look.

However without the colour control of dark radiating spars, the whole would have been too bright and confused to have been successful. Similarly, by controlling the colour of the rim and bringing that same hue into the hub, there was a small amount of cohesion which enabled the end result to work.

Colour plate 7 also shows the random use of colour. Here fairly long lengths of the same type of yarns were knotted together and worked into the top. Yes, knotted!

It was possible to do this because the yarn had a knop in it and contained irregular colour and uneven texture throughout. Being a cotton, it stayed firm so the knots remained hard lumps in the actual work. By knotting two pieces of yarn together where it was thinner, the knot was unnoticeable. A further factor in avoiding detection was to work two strands together increasing the unevenness of colour and texture.

This top was the result of a visit to a mill shop where a bag of thrums was purchased. The length of the strands of yarn was between one and three metres. First the strands were looped over a coathanger and then pulled out to be knotted and wound into a ball. Inevitably there was some selection made in an unconscious way. Initially the top was intended to be a truly haphazard selection but due to habits gained over the last years of observing nature there was an unconscious use of the strands that took the paler and bluer tones to the top, keeping the bolder and stronger tones for the base. The final result is perhaps how a suburban garden would look if the eyes were filled with tears.

Figure 22 *Tailored shapings of the bodice emphasise*
the fullness of the chevron skirt

Figure 23 *A workshop project illustrating random colour controlled by quiet areas*

Knotted teenage top (Diagram 63)

Size
To fit chest: 71–76 cm (28–30 in). Length 31 cm (12 in).

Materials
Approx. 250 g of a cotton-type multi-coloured knop yarn. Two balls worked together to provide a thickness between DK and Aran. (Argyll's Cotton-on would work if you cannot obtain oddments.)
5.00 mm hook.

Diagram 63 Teenage top using colours at random

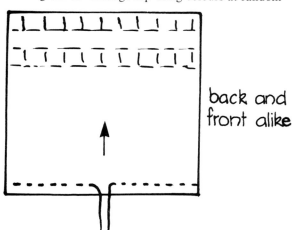

back and front alike

Tension
11 sts to 10 cm (4 in) worked over trebles.

To make
Work 88 ch.
Row 1 1 tr in 4th ch from hook, 1 tr in each ch to end, join with ss (NB: Watch the foundation row does not twist), 3 ch, turn. (86 sts)
Work 6 rows in tr.
Divide for yoke:
 First half:
Row 8 42 tr, 3 ch, turn. (43 sts)
Work 6 rows tr on these 43 sts.
Row 15 1 ch (making 4 in all with 3 turning ch) * miss 1 st, 1 tr in next st, 1 ch, rep from * 19 times, 1 tr in last st, 3 ch, turn.
Row 16 *1 tr in ch sp, 1 tr on tr, rep from * to end.
Repeat rows 15 and 16 twice and row 15 once. Break off yarn.
 Second half:
Rejoin yarn to next st on 8th row and work as for first half.
Join shoulders by connecting 8 sts on each side. These can be sewn or crocheted together.
Base row Rejoin yarn to foundation chain and work a row of 1 dc, 1 ch, using every alternate chain.
Make a tie of 125 cm (49 in) using two or three strands together. Thread this through the holes just made, commencing at centre front.

4. Use of vivid colours

The bold use of colours as in a child's painting or as produced in the ethnic artforms of hot climates where there is colourful and bright flora and fauna, is quite stimulating. The need to think of 'toning down' or 'giving lift' can be ignored and the results are usually dramatic and effective. On the whole there is a bright 'happiness' about the finished item that is transmitted to the onlooker. This way of using colour is just one stage on from a totally random choice. The following points should be considered.

a the overall effect should have a quiet period in it somewhere so that the colours do not jangle on the eyes to make the picture blur. The quiet patch is often obtained by using the one colour that is the least dramatic when placed next to ALL the other colours being used. A block of this tone amongst the busy usage of the others creates a place of quiet stillness that helps in the use of vivid colours and tones. Colour plate 3 shows a waistcoat made (on and off) by Joan Hadwin over a period of 18 months. The original waistcoat was inspired by looking at a book of embroidery. Joan's painstaking approach to all her work saw her first make a large selection of flowers from crepe wool, using many colours. Although the wool was 4-ply, Joan split the yarn down so that she was working with only one or two strands out of the original four at any one time. Some flowers had contrasting edges, others had a flower mounted on a flower. An embroidery needle was used on others to make a bold inner line. Next came a body shape on which to pin and arrange the motifs. Crocheted leaves in the same 4-ply crepe wool, was once more split into single or double strands and used to soften the vividness of the flower heads. Much re-arranging was necessary to finally obtain natural blocks and curves of colour. The quiet period in all this kaleidoscope of colour was vital. Once balance was achieved, Joan felt she did not like the background of the iron-on cotton showing through and meticulously covered the whole of the remaining spaces (however small or large) with embroidery chain stitch, using two strands of the split wool in greens. The final stage was a lining of a different shade of iron-on cotton, finishing with a border of double crochet using the yarn in its natural state.

b Simple block type stitch patterns are useful using strong colours. The poncho on page 52 (figure 15) is an excellent example of bright hues being worked in bands and blocks.

c A popular use of primary and/or bright colours is in the making of the 'granny' square knee and bed blankets. (See page 46, figure 12.) The colours used can be as haphazard and vivid as can be and if the last row of each motif is worked in the same tone, and then all the square motifs joined together with that tone, there is an overall effect that is most cheering.

d If, for the first time, the use of bright colours is worrying, try adding it afterwards as shown in the bolero on page 55 (figure 17). (See Section E, Surface crochet.)

There are occasions when it is essential to use the brightest and most garish colours that can be found. The beret on page 55 is an example of this. The white/pale network of chains in a fluffy yarn forms the main beret shape and softens the under colours, intensity. If the colours used for the underlay were not vivid the final result would be pale and insipid. As it is the underlay tones just blend into the network of the main shape.

Maggi Jo Norton is known for her colourful motifs. Given below (see figure 24) is one of her sweater designs. Strong colour is an integral part of Maggi Jo's whole approach to crochet and this sweater provides a useful illustration of how to be bold, yet controlled.

Maggi Jo's flower design jumper
(Diagram 64, figure 24)

Size
To fit a medium bust.

Materials
Approx. 200 g of DK smooth yarn in six colours: A = pale colour; B = medium colour; C = dark colour; D = bright colour; E = 1st pale mohair; F = 2nd pale mohair.
4.50 mm hook.

Tension
Approx. 3 sts to 2.5 cm (1 in) over straight rows. Large motif = 12.5 cm (5 in) diameter. Small motif = 9 cm (4 in) diameter.
The body section consists of 15 small motifs, 9 large motifs and one corn motif panel. Sleeve sections are made of the cloud motif measuring 130 cm × 15 cm (51 in × 6 in).

Corn motif of body
This is worked sideways and should measure 102 cm long (40 in) by 25 cm wide (10 in).

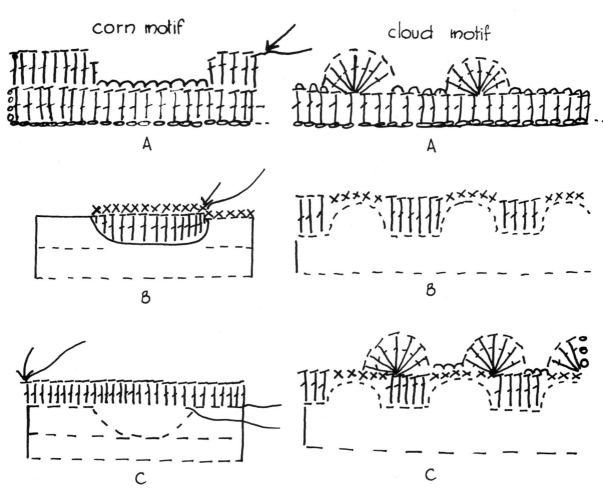

corn motif   cloud motif

A   A

B   B

C   C

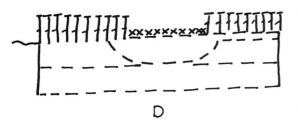

D

Diagram 64 Maggi Jo's sweater pattern (final shape and stitches of motifs)

Use the two mohairs and the bright DK for the actual corn, with the other three DK yarns for the background.

1. Make a ch of 27.
2. 1 tr in 3rd ch from hook, 1 tr in each ch to end, 3 ch, turn. (25 sts)

3. 4 tr, 13 ss, tr to end. Fasten off 1st yarn. DO NOT TURN.
4. Join 2nd colour to top of turning ch, 6 dc, 12 tr, 1 ss, turn.
5. 12 dc, fasten off 2nd colour.
6. With corn stalk on left, join in 3rd colour at RH edge where 1st colour was finished.
7. 3 ch, 4 tr, 1 dc in first dc of corn cob, 11 dc, 1 tr into first dc of corn stalk, 5 tr (end of row), turn.
8. Continue motif pattern with 3 ch, 7 tr, 11 ss, 4 tr. Fasten off. Repeat pattern from step 4. Always begin corn stalk on turning ch of previous row.

The size of the corn cob and stalk is varied by the number of trebles in step 8 (or 3). More trebles make the corn cob shorter. Conversely less trebles and more slip stitches make the corn cob longer. (NB: There should be the same number of stitches in each row.)

To complete body piece
After working step 7, finish with 3 ch, tr to end of row. Fasten off.

Figure 24 Maggi Jo's motif sweater

Large flower motif

1. Using mohair E, 3 ch, join into a ring with ss, 1 ch, 7 dc into the ring. Join with ss to top of 1 ch. Fasten off.
2. Join in C, 1 ch, 2 dc in each of next 4 sts. * 1 ss, 2 ch, 1 tr in ss, rep from * twice, finishing at the beginning of round, 1 ss. Fasten off.
3. Join E in top of last petal. Make five shells as follows: *2 ch, 2 tr 1 ss, ss in same st, ss next st, rep from * 4 times finishing at top of petal made in C. Fasten off.
4. Join A in last st, * 1 dc, 2 tr in base of next sp, 2 dc on top of next petal, rep from * once, 4 dc, ** 2 tr into base of next sp, 2 dc on top of next petal. Rep from ** 3 times, 3 dc on top of next two joined petals, ss to join. Fasten off.
5. Join D to end of last round. Work approx. 10 to 12 dc along round. Fasten off. This should be an arc matching previous dark DK petals.

6. Using F, * work 2 ch, 3 tr, 1 ss in same st, miss 2 sts, rep from *. Fasten off.
7. Join in E, * miss 2 sts, work 2 ch, 3 tr, 1 ss in same st, rep from * 5 times. (NB: A full round should be completed.) Fasten off.
8. Join C in side of top left-hand petal and work 2 tr in each sp between shells, and 3 dc on top of shells, ss to beg. Fasten off. Motif is now complete.

Small flower motif

Use yarns E and F alternately for centres of these motifs. The surround is made with 3 DK yarns.

1. 3 ch, join in ring with ss, 3 ch, 8 tr join with ss to 3 ch.
2. 3 ch, 1 tr, ss into base of st. * ss into next st, 1 tr, ss in same st, rep from * to end, join with ss. Fasten off.
3. Join B to top of a petal, with WS facing. Put 2 tr bet petals, and 1 dc on top of petals. Fasten off.
4. Join in either C or D. * 2 dc, 2 dc in next st, rep from * to end, join with ss.

This mohair flower has 5 petals.

Finishing the body section

Stitch motifs tog as follows:
Sew large motifs tog with 8 cm joins so that they form a strip. Work two rows tr into gaps between flowers, increasing as required so that the strip measures 13 cm evenly all the way along. Fasten ends. Sew small motifs tog with 6 cm joins to form a strip. Using A, work 2 tr in each sp between motifs. Fasten ends. Strip should measure 9 cm evenly all the way along.

Sleeves

These two pieces are a back and a front which incorporate the top body part of the jumper. Use all six colours.

Back

Make 172 ch.
Row 1 1 tr in 4th ch from hook, tr to end. (169 sts) (137 cm)
Work *cloud* motif for 15 cm. The ends of this long strip are the cuffs.
After 2 rows change colour.
Row 2 Make shell stitch at irregular intervals along next row, using ss to separate the shells, i.e. make one shell of 5–7 trebles, 3 ss to next shell, 1 shell, 5 ss, etc. Fasten off 1st colour. Join second colour in same place.
Row 3 Return along row by dc in top 3 sts of each shell, work treble into ss of previous row.
Row 4 As row 2.
Repeat rows 3 and 4 with third colour.
Continue until work is required size, finishing on row 4.

Make sure that the shell stitches are irregularly placed above each other by using different sized spaces between each shell stitch row of each new colour.

Decreasing on sleeves is done from cuff edge. Measure 33 cm from both cuff edges. Mark with thread. Work two rows of cloud motif between these two points. There is no neck shaping on back of sleeve/body length.

Measure 41 cm from cuff edges and mark as before. Work two rows of cloud motif between these points. Measure 48 cm from both cuffs, and work two rows cloud motifs between these points. Fasten off.

On the last row of decreasing, work in treble.

Front

Work as back until decreasing.

Mark 10 cm either side of centre of last row worked on this strip for neck opening. On either side of the neck opening, work decreasing as on back, turning at neck edge. Keep the turn at the neck edge straight.

Finishing the jumper

Sew body pieces together to form a tube. Mark for sides. Sew sleeves together for 43 cm measured from each cuff, on bottom straight edge. Sew straight middle section of sleeve/body pieces onto the body of the jumper. The jumper should measure 51 cm across at this point.

Sew tops of sleeves together matching the decreases. Work 5 rows dc round neck, cuffs and hem.

Weave in all ends on back of work.

5. Illusion of colour

The use of blendings and changing colour in crochet is extremely easy as only one ball of coloured yarn need ever be used at any one time in any one row to produce a huge variety of effects. The ability to insert the hook in places other than the tops of stitches and still not cause any tension or mathematical problems, gives the crochet worker great freedom to design and use colour.

For instance a pale yarn can be used to encroach upon a strong stripe of colour made by the previous row and vice versa thus softening or deepening the effect of the colour.

Jane's poncho (Diagram 65, figure 15 on page 52)

At no time was more than one colour used on any one row in the poncho. The poncho commenced with a square of a single colour, starting at the centre. Three

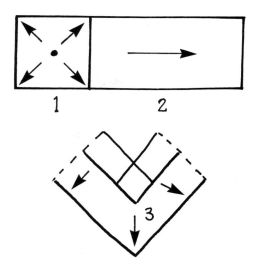

Diagram 65 Jane's poncho

bands of colour made a strong border to the open motif; the use of a double crochet row in the darkest shade acted as a frame but without dominating the square. Several rows of double crochet in the first colour increased the square to a suitable size for the central diamond.

The back and front were worked at the same time.

The next stage was to make a strip of coloured crochet that would go from one of the upper sides of the diamond, over the shoulder to meet the other diamond (2). As both pieces were being worked together this meant that once the two strips were joined, a deep border of colour could be worked round the poncho as a square (3), using some of the colour bands in the original strips to keep a cohesive whole.

After the double crochet rows of the original square (1), the strip was started with dropped double crochet used at the end of the poncho (worked by inserting the hook in rows lower down than the one in progress and then lifting the yarn to the level of the row being worked so that the yarn did not gather the fabric). This not only modified the overall look of the colour band being worked but created a geometrical pattern. (See diagram 66 which shows how four rows of double crochet in one colour is changed by using different lengths of dropped double crochet stitches.)

Three strips of colour were worked in the paler shade followed by a dark band and a light band of colour. The next dark band used quadruple trebles to encroach over the pale band to form boxes.

The use of the dropped and raised long trebles (as described in the blending of colours in *Creative Design*

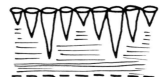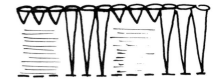

Diagram 66 Some possible places to insert the hook when working dropped double crochet to change the visual shape of a contrasting stripe

in Crochet) can be used to good effect to create all kinds of colour blending. The length of the treble is determined on a sample tension piece so that it is possible to anchor the long treble round the stem of the treble in the row of matching colour three rows down. Thus the long treble lies on top of the contrasting band but once the stitch is completed the yarn is in its rightful place at the top of the stitches being worked. Many of the stripes used interesting stitch combinations which softens the hardness of strong geometric lines.

Finally a deep polo neck was made using raised treble rib.

Rather like Mary Davies and her Polish Star stitch cushions, when Jane came to classes she had only made granny squares and this was her first fashion garment. As the poncho and the cushions do not rely on a perfect fit, both items were ideal as starter projects, however adventurous the stitches and colour combinations.

The same techniques can be used in mohair. The long hairs softening the stripe effect even further, as in the beret on page 21 (figure 4).

The multi-coloured use of long trebles as shown in the colour plate 4, opposite page 48 of *Creative Design in Crochet* is a further example of encroaching stitches which give the illusion of interlaced colour bands when in reality they were rows of single colours.

Mohair beret (figure 4)

Size

To fit average head.

Materials

Scraps of mohair in different shades and hues (approximately 5 g per colour); a main neutral colour, used on alternate rows which produces a softening effect to the whole overall appearance.
Size 6.00 mm hook.

To make

With an oddment make 3 ch, join into a ring with ss.
Rnd 1 1 ch, 7 dc in ring, join with ss, fasten off.
Rnd 2 In main colour, 3 ch, 2 tr in each dc, join with ss. (16 sts) This yarn can remain attached.
Rnd 3 With another oddment work 1 dc in each st to end, join with ss. Fasten off.
Rnd 4 With neutral still attached, work into the base of the stitches in rnd 3 so that the neutral is worked into rnd 2. 3 ch, 1 tr in same place, 2 tr in each st to end. (32 sts)
Rnd 5 With an oddment, 1 ch, *1 dropped dc (insert hook into base of tr on rnd 4) 1 dc, rep from * to end, 1 dropped dc before joining with ss. (NB: Pull dropped dcs up to level of other dc or rnd 4 will buckle.) Fasten off. (See diagram 66.)
Rnd 6 With neutral, 3 ch, 2 tr, *2 tr in next st, 3 tr, rep from * to last st, 2 tr in last st, join with ss.
Rnd 7 With oddment, 1 ch, *1 RtrF, 1 dc, rep from * to last st, 1 RtrF, join with ss, fasten off.
Rnd 8 With neutral, 3 ch, 3 tr, *2 tr in next st, 4 tr, rep from * to last st, 2 tr in last st, join with ss.
Rnd 9 With an oddment that is large enough to do approx 3 rounds, work 1 row dc, join with ss. Fasten off.
Rnd 10 With neutral, 3 ch, 4 tr, *2 tr in next st, 5 tr, rep from * to last st, 2 tr in last st, join with ss.
Before working round 11, use a small oddment and work over all the stitches in rnd 8 using the tambour method of surface crochet (see page 93).
Fasten off.
Work in exactly the same way with another coloured oddment, over rnd 10. Fasten off.
Rnd 11 With the same yarn as that used in rnd 9 work 1 ch, 1 dc, *1 RdtrF into dc of same colour on rnd 9, 2 dc, rep from * to last st, 1 RdtrF, join with ss.
(NB: As this is a circle and an increase row has been made, there are not sufficient stitches to miss 2 sts at base of raised dtr. Sometimes 2 will be missed and sometimes 1 – try to keep this uniform.)
Rnd 12 With neutral, 3 ch, 1 tr in each st to end, join with ss.
Rnd 13 With oddment * 1 tr, 1 ss, rep from * to end, fasten off.

Rnd 14 With neutral, 3 ch, * tr 2 tog, 3 tr, rep from * to end. Fasten off.

Rnd 15 With oddment, *dc 2 tog, 4 dc, rep from * to end. Fasten off. (NB: Adjust to fit head bet rnds 12–15.)

Return to centre of beret and with RS facing, join in an oddment, (1 ch, 1 htr, 1 dc, 1 ss) 4 times round centre inside the 3rd rnd. Fasten off. With another oddment working directly into the very centre of the 2 cup shapes made, work 1 very large (or 3 small) puff stitches (see page 38). Break off yarn.

Fasten in all ends.

A good illustration of what is meant by the illusion of colour is for a piece of material, such as a length of tweed containing more than one colour, to be taken to a wool shop to find a yarn to make a matching garment. Often the temptation is to pick out one of the threads woven into the fabric but when taken out in isolation, the colour would be harsh and uncompromising, not complementing the material at all. Really look at a piece of beautiful woven fabric and note how many different brightly coloured threads have been used. For instance a brown or jade green tweed that is quite deep in toning from a distance will often contain the brightest of pure orange hue, or purple, etc. A bright orange top may be exactly what is being looked for but usually it is something that is less brilliant and more in keeping with the overall effect that is wanted.

Nature is a mistress at this sort of thing. One only has to look at a leaf, a group of rocks, a tree, to realise all the colours of the rainbow can be incorporated into it when the sun shines, or the rain has washed over it. A bird we think of as starkly black and white, the magpie, has vibrant sea-green tail feathers.

6. Looking at nature

Once the experiment of using coloured yarns begins, there is a tendency to want to progress and 'paint with yarn'. A longing grows to use the versatility of stitch combinations, with the many beautiful shades on the market. Just going into a well-stocked wool shop gives a crochet worker 'itchy fingers'.

Endless suggestions can be provided by nature itself. I can outline here only a few of the innumerable ways to use what you have observed. You may, for instance, want to *reproduce* what your eyes see.

Method of working a scene in crochet

1. Look at the whole scene. Some vistas are easy to reproduce in crochet using small quantities of fashion yarns carefully chosen to give the effect of hills, sky, meadows, etc. (See figure 28 as an example.)

2. Choose the shape and make a paper replica to the actual size. The example given in diagram 67 below is a waistcoat with an asymmetrical base line.

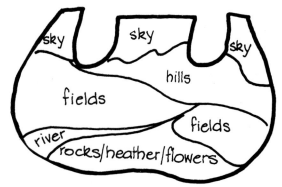

Diagram 67 Waistcoat shape broken into blocks of colour to be crocheted as a base for final detail

3. Choose an overall idea and simplify it into main outlines as shown. Draw these lines onto the prepared shape.

4. Select the yarns remembering that if the waistcoat is not to be lined, the thicker, heavier, least elastic yarns have to be used at the top to take the physical weight of the rest of the design. This is not so easy in the example given as the sky should be light and feathery. One way is to work the design without hanging during the making and then finish the garment off with an iron-on fabric. Alternatively use yarns that are physically heavy at the top but have an illusion of lightness, whilst at the base of the waistcoat the yarns can be physically light but with an illusion of heaviness. The waistcoat in the final chapter of *Creative Design in Crochet* does the latter, as the rocks and bird outlines are of lightweight washable suede which does not pull against the yarns worked to create sea and sky.

5. Now decide whether the crochet is being worked from top to bottom, bottom to top or even sideways. Make the necessary foundation chain working one block of simplified colour at a time. For instance if working the example given, and working from bottom to top, the foundation

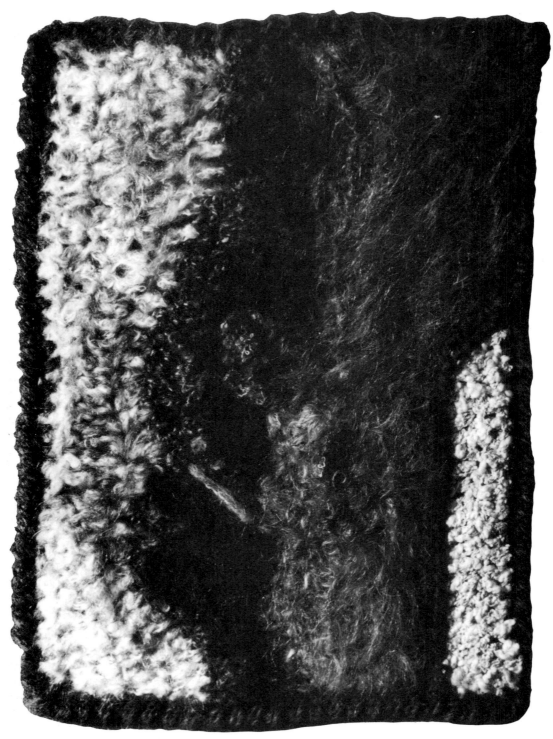

Figure 25 *Collage using textured yarns to obtain the creative use of colour: this black and white print highlights the yarn changes*

chain would be for the section of rocks/ heather/flowers. The shape of this area is worked in total. Next work the fields, connecting the work as it progresses rather than making individual blocks and having to put them together with ugly joins (see page 58 for additional points of technique).

6. Once the blocks are worked and connected together extra detail can be given by surface crochet.
7. Working curves into a design needs more stitches at the top edge of a curve and less at the bottom or depression part. This is rather like the principles used in chevron designs.
8. To help stitches remain flat in irregular rows of varying stitch heights it may be necessary to increase the number of stitches where there are tall stitches and decrease the number of stitches where there are short stitches.
9. Blocks of areas can be in a medium other than crochet, as mentioned previously. Suede, leather, knitting, woven fabric, etc. give a very good effect.
10. If any stiffness is to be incorporated into a garment design, extra notice will have to be taken of the roundness and fullness of the figure by using darts, adding a movement allowance, or even adding turnings.
11. If a picture design is going round the body figure, it is usually better to work the whole design in one flat piece rather than attempt working in a tube, unless you are a trained or experienced artist. It is only too easy to get the balance and proportion wrong if the whole 'picture' cannot be seen at once.

Where to look for suitable designs

1) Embroidery books, as these often use a simple outline. Diagram 68 shows an example of this.

Diagram 68 Simple embroidery outlines can be used for crochet textures

2) Children's books, which again are usually drawn without too much detail and with strong outlines. In particular the books that teach very young children rather than the beautiful, almost 'coffee-table' books which have at long last become available. From the second group *we* can learn about colour mixing!
3) Embroidery transfer sheets, but choose these carefully as some of them can be very detailed.
4) Nature books for colour blending. Here the simplification will have to be done by you.
5) Photographs. Try tracing over the main areas to give you an idea of the shapes of the basic blocks that will be needed to produce the design.
6) Books on the fine arts.
7) Just by making a little time to 'stand and stare' so that you can observe life itself.

A close inspection of a tiny bit of nature can result in fascinating details. The many shapes of cells seen under a microscope can be reproduced in delightful interlocking ways.

One of the finest crochet workers to use a lifetime's experience of close contact through a microscope is Kathleen Basford. Kathleen took up crochet after an early retirement as a geneticist. She then mastered with characteristic thoroughness the techniques of crochet as they came into her sphere of working. Because she had the time to play she incorporated her own life's considerable skills in the area of colour crochet. Her years of closely observing nature gave her the ability to reproduce (with lots of trial and error and pulling out!) what she saw. Colour plate 1 shows one of her garments, and figure 26 shows a close-up of another. (See Section E.) Now she has decided to postpone colour crochet for some years to concentrate on mastering the techniques of 'lace' crochet and knitting.

Patchwork sweater (colour plate 6)

The techniques of linking stitches of one block to another (page 58) can be used to produce an irregular patchwork of colour either as part of a collage or as a sweater (see figure 27).

One method of achieving this effect is to chart the colours on a graph paper. Below, diagram 69 denotes the stitches and rows needed for the sweater both on squared graph paper and crochet graph paper. It also shows the order in which the blocks were worked.
1. Work a tension square using the main yarn.
2. Next decide how many stitches are required for the width.

Figure 26 *Inspired by larch and lichen from a branch found in Wales (Kathleen Basford)*

Figure 27 *Patchwork blocks: as each colour is worked separately and linked to its neighbour there are no ugly joins*

3. Work out how many rows to stitches are needed (e.g. two treble rows to three stitches). Alternatively use the correct crochet graph paper.
4. Use different symbols for the different yarns.
5. Work to the graph using one yarn at a time.
Work another piece for the other side of the body.
Join side seams.
Using a heavily textured yarn, work 1 row dc round armhole edges, neck and hem.

Tension: 2 stitches wide = 1 stitch high

- • Yarn A
- / Yarn B
- □ Yarn C
- o Yarn D

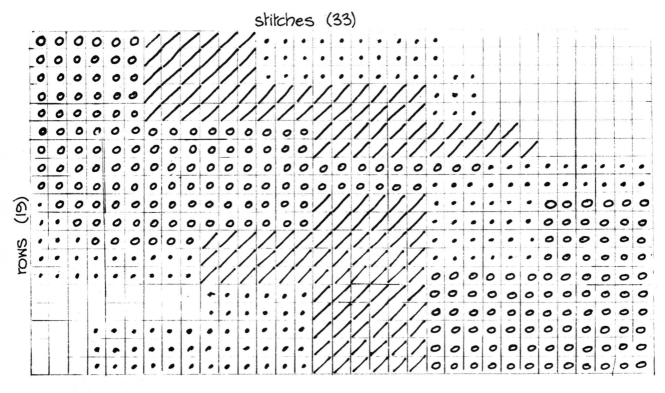

stitches (33)

rows (19)

Diagram 69 Equal sized squared paper. (Crochet graph paper on which 2 stitches wide = 1 stitch high is now available.)

You could also, of course, *change* what your eyes see. That is, looking at what is directly in front of you and taking note of the shapes, the colour blocks and use the *ideas* that the stone wall, hills, patchwork fields, etc. can inspire. It may be that the clouds forming shadows on a sunlit scene will influence a choice of colour; it may be the lace patterns of winter trees against a brilliant sunset or dawn sky; or it may simply be the pattern of a spot of oil in a puddle.

The photograph of the 'scene in a ring', shown in figure 28 was based on hills covered in bracken on a late autumn day when the sky was bright but overcast with thin cloud. The idea of working in the ring came after looking at a weaving exhibition. (See Section F, page 105.)

Another way of looking but changing entirely what one sees, is to use just the colours that are included in any single petal or leaf as the colour theme for a garment or piece of collage, etc. This often leads the observer to experiment with colours that would not normally have been included until the close look at nature had been made. The thought of using orange, tinted clear reds and bluish pinks in strong tones would have made me shudder at one time. However, as can be seen in the colour plate 4, if small amounts are judiciously used, such a colour combination really works. Two factors were responsible for me persevering with this colour combination; one was the beautiful coral photographed by Jacques Cousteau and the other was Bernat Klein as he generously spoke about his personal view of colour and the way he looked towards nature whenever he needed inspiration for a new yarn or fabric. (See 'Surface crochet', page 93 for technique.)

Figure 28 *Fun project worked in a ring: impressionistic reproduction of autumn hills*

7. Effect of light

Against a window, or a mirror, any article is going to have light either shining through it or reflected through it and should be worked with the daylight in front of the crochet worker so that it can be held up periodically and inspected in the same light as it will normally be viewed. The effect of different types of light onto a fabric is dramatic. One only has to think of how the colour of clothes changes under street lighting; notice how the detail fades from an article when placed against a window; think of the effect of different coloured lights on a stage set in the theatre, to realise light *is* an important consideration.

To obtain the very best results for the item being made, select the materials by the light in which it is most likely to be seen. Work the project with frequent checks in that light to make certain it is working to the desired effect. When the item is completed leave it for a few days before giving it a final critical look – again in the light that it is going to be seen by most. For a fixture such as a curtain or a collage it is preferable to hang it up before the finishing touches are made.

8. Final thoughts on colour

It is impossible to cover the use of colour in depth. Should colour in crochet interest you then use the libraries, art galleries, nature documentaries on TV, etc. to give insight and begin the logical sequence of hard work that has been inspired. It has been said that 'anything goes'. Colour is a personal taste and the individual's characteristics and lifestyle will affect what is felt to be 'good colour sense'. If what you are making is for someone else, however, it is perhaps not the best thing to inflict your own personal taste upon them. So look and listen for clues as to what they imagine and actually want. Usually a mixture of 'them' and 'us' produces the satisfactory outcome of a well-designed, well-made article that is well-received!

Section E
Surface crochet

Surface crochet can be worked on any material: knitting, woven fabrics, crochet, etc., are all possible bases for supporting the crochet worked on top of the base fabric. The textile used should be sufficiently strong and not pull out of shape with the physical weight of the crochet being added.

There are two main ways of doing the surface crochet:

1. using the tambour method of embroidery;
2. crocheting all kinds of stitches freely onto any surface that will accommodate the hook being inserted into it.

1. The tambour method

This method is worked with the yarn placed beneath the fabric. The hook is inserted from above into the base material poking through to the underside and collecting the yarn from below the fabric before pulling it up to the surface (diagram 70). Only a chain stitch can be made using this method, but interesting effects can be obtained by making the chains of irregular length. In particular this method of working surface crochet is useful for:

Diagram 70 Tambour method of surface crochet

a outlining;
b tracery effects between motifs;
c underlining in colour;
d colour blending and softening;
e adding detail to an area that requires a flat and untextured look;
f an effective way of using random-dyed bouclé or other textured yarns, simply;
g if the base material can only take a lightweight design.

Evening outfit (Figure 29)

Here is a simple use of this kind of crochet.

First A long line sleeveless waistcoat was made in double crochet using a 4-ply cotton chenille (the kind most likely to be obtained in a machine knitting shop supplying yarns to the public).

Second Before the shoulder seams were joined a newspaper template was made.

Third A rough pencil sketch was then put into the template and the final thoughts were boldly outlined with a felt tip.

Fourth This outline was copied free-hand, the 'template' being placed on the carpet for easy reference. (Those with animals or children, blue-tack to the wall or pin to the curtain out of reach!)

Fifth The multi-facetted glass sequins that had been mirror-plated, were firmly stitched to the whole. This last stage proved the most difficult as the centre of the glass cut the sewing threads when the sequins were being applied.

Jacket

The tree motif on the back of the jacket (see figure 30) uses the same method of working crochet detail. The surface crochet here seems quite textured in com-

Figure 29 *Evening outfit in cotton chenille, the sleeveless jacket using surface crochet and beading with mirror-backed glass sequins. Inspired by Japanese flower arranging*

Figure 30 *Textured yarns used to add the tree design to a classic jacket*

parison to the evening waistcoat. However the only difference is in the choice of yarns. The main yarn was an oddment found in a bargain basket without a label. It was tightly plied in parts with large soft slubs between. The colours ranged from light grey to pewter with a twist of a moleskin colour dotted here and there. Towards the base of the trunk deep 'wet' moss green was used. On the upper edges of most of the branches a very pale, cold, blue-grey chenille was added to give the illusion of strong day-light catching the branches. A final touch was a spider's web in 10's crochet cotton. (The base of the jacket is Tunisian crochet, unfortunately a branch of crochet not covered in this book!)

The centre panel of the evening jacket featured on the back cover also uses this technique; as does the skirt illustrated in colour plate 4.

Skirt (colour plate 4)

1) A paper template is first made based on the hip and waist measurements (see diagram 71). This is an 8-gore skirt and so the waist of 72 cm (28 in) was divided by 8, which is 9 cm (3½ in).
2) Decide how wide the crochet strips which join the panels are to be. In this case, 4 cm (1½ in).
3) Deduct this amount from each panel evenly, here we have a final measure of 5 cm (2 in).
4) Work the same way for the hip measure. In this case 96 (38 in) i.e. 96 ÷ 8 = 12 − 4 = 8 cm (3¼ in).
5) Transfer these measures to the paper to make the template. It is more accurate to draw a vertical line to mark the centre of the panel and then place the calculations evenly either side of the line drawn. At the top of the line, mark in the waist which in the example is 5 cm (2 in). 15 cm (6 in) down, evenly mark in the hip measure. It is appreciated that in some dress designers' view this is a little high for the hip, but there are quite a lot of ladies with the fullness of the hips higher than average and even with those ladies who have an average measure, the extra fullness only adds elegance to the completed skirt.
6) Mark in the length of the skirt minus 3 cm (approx. 1 in) for the waistband and final border.
7) Draw a line from waist to hip to hem on either side of the vertical line. This line should measure the same as that marked on the perpendicular. Now draw an even curve from the side lines to the central line to give the scallop edge as shown.
8) Cut eight panels from a woven material or alterna-

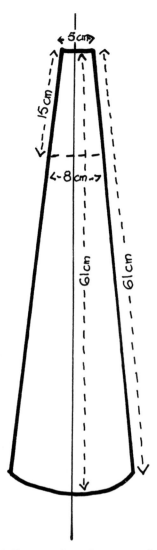

Diagram 71 Construction of a pattern for a panelled skirt

tively knit or crochet a fairly smooth panel to fit the template now made. The material used in the illustrated skirt was Bernat Klein's mohair – a loose-weave bouclé fabric in loop mohair. Should it be necessary, overlock the edges on a sewing machine or hand sew with an oversewing stitch.

9) Using a variety of heavily textured yarns work round the panel on both sides and on the waist edge. Only one row of dc and a Crab stitch was worked at the hem and this was added after the skirt had been assembled completely.

10) When the three sides measure 2 cm ($\frac{3}{4}$ in), work the other panels the same.

11) At this stage with each panel framed by the colours of the border it is a sensible time to decide on whether any surface crochet is to be worked onto the original panels. In the example just two panels had surface crochet which picked up the colours of the border yarns and gave an exclusive touch to the whole garment. A plain panel was placed between the two panels that had had the surface crochet worked on them. This plain panel then determined the front of the skirt.

12) Join the panels together using a textured yarn and Crab stitch on the right side to carry through the texture in the borders.

13) Complete the waist with extra rows if necessary and adding any of the following: zip, draw-string, elastic, lightweight belt backing.

14) Complete the hem.

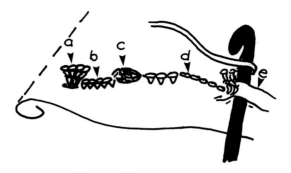

Diagram 72 Surface crochet: (a) Free standing; (b) Line of double crochet; (c) Treble cluster anchored flat with a slip stitch; (d) Loose chain; (e) Insertion of hook through the fabric

2. Textured surface crochet

This method of surface crochet is worked by having the yarn on top of the fabric. The hook is inserted from above as in the tambour method, but the fabric is 'pinched' so that a whole stem of a crochet stitch, or a few fibres of woven cloth, can be used to anchor the crochet and the hook emerges still on the right side of the fabric. (See diagram 72.)

A crocheted fabric can be made with surface crochet in mind. Raised treble or double treble ridges being a good example. (See front cover.) The following pattern is based on raised double trebles.

Waistcoat with surface crochet stripes
(Diagram 73, figure 31)

Size

87 cm (34 in) bust. Repeat rows 2 and 3 once more at ** for each additional size increase. Back length 57 cm ($22\frac{1}{2}$ in).

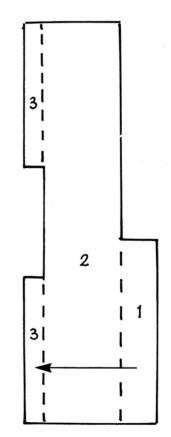

Diagram 73 Waistcoat in raised double trebles with surface crochet on ridges in crab stitch

Figure 31 *Crab stitch added afterwards to the ridges of the raised double treble fabric – a useful way to use up those tiny scraps of textured fashion yarn*

Materials

350 g DK (Patons Beehive was used) for base; oddments of colour for the Crab stitch ridges.
4.50 mm crochet hook. (NB: If this makes fabric stiff use a 5.00 mm hook.)

Tension

3 sts to 2 cm (¾ in) measured over smooth side of raised dtr fabric.

First side (includes front and back)

Make 175 ch.

Row 1 1 dtr in 5th ch from hook, 1 dtr in each ch to end, 3 ch, turn (1 ch less than plain dtr as hook is inserted lower down). (172 sts)*

Row 2 1 RdtrF round each st to end, 3 ch, turn.

Row 3 1 RdtrB round each st to end, 3 ch, turn. **

Rep rows 2 and 3, 5 times.

On the first 82 sts rep rows 2 and 3 twice and then row 2 once more.

Fasten off.

SPECIAL NOTE: This pattern has a natural bias. If it becomes too acute the garment will not hang correctly.

Second side

As first side to *.

Work row 3 and row 2 – this reverses the sides.

On first 82 sts work row 3 once and then rows 2 and 3 twice. Fasten off.

(NB: Larger sizes may prefer an underarm gusset of 2–3 rows using 40 sts.)

Using an oddment of colour, Crab stitch the centre backs together on the right side. Fasten off.

Work colourful rows of Crab stitch using the chain tops of the stitches left in working raised double trebles. Darn in all the ends.

Side edge

Work 1 dc in each foundation ch to end, 1 ch, turn.

Work 3 more rows of dc.

Join underarm with RS facing and main colour, in Crab st over 40 sts.

Continue in Crab st round the armhole opening.

Front and neck border

Work 1 dc in each st of fronts with 2 dc in each row end at back neck.

Dec 1 st at each side of back neck on every row for a good fit.

Work 5 rows of dc.

Finish with RS facing to work 1 row Crab st.

Welt

Join main yarn to base of front edge with RS facing. Make 2 dc in each row end adjusting at dc borders as necessary.

Work 2 rows dc.

Finish with 1 row Crab stitch and RS facing. Fasten off.

Variation

Use a very soft mohair worked on the same hook, of 4-ply rather than a DK thickness. Using the tambour method of surface crochet, work over the stitches between the ridges, using an equally lightweight mohair to create shadows, and a variety of discreet and subtle shadings.

Before discussing the 'free-form' use of surface crochet it may be wise to list some of the disadvantages of surface crochet in general.

3. Points to watch when working surface crochet

1) If the background is very close and an 'all-over' pattern of surface crochet is added, it could result in a very stiff item. Good for collage perhaps but not always suitable in fashion.
2) The physical weight of dense and solid surface crochet makes a fashion garment very heavy and cumbersome to wear.
3) If the stitches in the background are a loose and open design areas of 'solid' or heavy crochet can draw some of the stitches together, forcing others to open. This distorts the background severely and unless specifically used in the design as a feature, should be carefully observed in order that steps to rectify the situation can be taken.
4) Even on a closely crocheted background, if the actual weight of the yarn being used in the surface work is heavier (that is a linen on an acrylic; or a closely spun wool chunky, on a 4-ply wool background) the weight of the parts covered by the surface work will drag against the unworked background fabric causing the article to be dragged down unevenly.

As with colour, the way you eventually use surface crochet is very personal. Possible ways of creating textured effects with this method are as follows:

a In a net mesh made of 1 tr, 1 ch, (preferably using a firm yarn such as jute or cotton) make regular folds

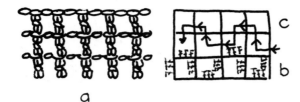

Diagram 74 'Portuguese' style crochet:
(a) Network of trebles and chains; (b) 'Snake' line of 3 trebles round each stem and chain space;
(c) Direction of surface crochet

or soft pleats of trebles. It is the regularity of the all-over pattern in 'Portuguese' crochet that makes it possible to work in such an open background. This design is suitable for table mats and floor rugs. (See diagram 74.)

b Place 8–12 trebles in the same place to form a free-standing 'cup'. Commence as though working in the round or for a row, with 3 ch. Join the trebles with a ss. Should the same yarn be needed close by, it is possible to ss down the turning chain to take the yarn from the top of the cup-shape to the level of the base fabric.

c 5 or 6 treble clusters anchored in one place with each cluster slip stitched down at the top, gives a large berry effect. 2 or 3 trebles worked in the same way give a leaf or petal effect. Clones knots also give the effects of flowers as in the child's bolero (figure 17, page 55).

d Stems or connecting lines can be made by:
   (i) small chain loops which are anchored only at each end (be careful not to make these too long or they will catch on door handles);
   (ii) ss, this is a good method for working along the side of a ridge in a fabric of raised trebles;
   (iii) double crochet (if the fabric is folded at the point(s) where the line is being made, it is quite easy to work the double crochet);
   (iv) Crab stitch.

e A seaweed effect can be made using short lengths of chain, to which picots of different sizes are added, and anchoring the picot looped chains at random.

f Flowers of individual petals can be made by putting 1 dc, 1 htr, 1 tr, 1 htr, 1 dc, 1 ss all into the same place and moving round the central spot with more of the petals. The outer petals can be made bigger by using either dtrs, or more trs, to make the petals larger in height or width.

g Irregular shapes can be made by using the different heights of the stitches and then adding another row of irregular height stitches in a different yarn or colour. This gives the effect of crunchy coral or ragged flower petals.

It is rarely possible to give explicit instructions for nature inspired art forms worked directly onto the fabric. However the bolero has only a simple pattern with the majority of the flower heads of Clones knots nestling in the part of the bolero where the three branches separate. The rest of the coloured flowers and buds are spread out along the branches but leaving much of the stems or branches free from further decoration. The strong greens chosen are sufficient by themselves in places on the contrasting white background.

Where buds are added, they really should be proportional in size and smaller than the flowers, going to even smaller buds as the stem tips are neared.

Child/teenager bolero (basic pattern) (Diagram 75)

A basic shape of trebles crocheted in mohair was made, as follows, before the surface crochet was added.

Materials

150 g 70% mohair and wool, of an Aran to DDK thickness. (Wendy Donna or Argyll Finesse)
7.00 mm hook.

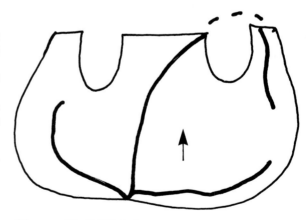

Diagram 75 Child's bolero

Figure 32 *Three-dimensional oddments can be arranged against a piece of driftwood to produce a free-standing sculpture*

To make
Make 26 ch
Row 1 1 tr in 4th ch from hook, 1 tr in each st to end, 3 ch, turn. (24 sts)
Row 2 1 tr in each st to end, 3 ch, turn.
Rep row 2, 9 times.
Row 12 1 tr in same place as turning ch (1 inc made) tr to last st, 2 tr in last st, 3 ch, turn.
Row 13 2 tr in same place as turning ch, tr to last st, 3 tr in last st (30 sts). Break off yarn before working 3 ch.

First front
Make 8 ch.
Row 1 1 tr in 4th ch from hook, 1 tr in each ch to end, 3 ch, turn. (6 sts)
Row 2 1 tr in each st to end, 3 ch, turn.
Row 3 As row 2.
Row 4 (inc row) 1 tr in same place as turning ch, tr to end, 3 ch, turn.

Repeat row 3 and 4, 3 times. Work row 4, 3 times. (13 sts)
Row 14 1 tr in same place as turning ch, tr to last st, 3 tr in last st, 3 ch, turn.
Row 15 2 tr in same place as turning ch, tr to last st, 2 tr in last st.
Break off yarn.

Second front
Make 8 ch.
Row 1 1 tr in 4th ch from hook, 1 tr in each ch to end, 3 ch, turn.
Row 2 1 tr in each st to end, 3 ch, turn.
Row 3 As row 2.
Row 4 (inc row) tr to last st, 2 tr in last st, 3 ch, turn.
Rep rows 3 and 4, 3 times. Work row 4, 3 times.
Row 14 2 tr in same place as turning ch, tr to last st, 2 tr in last st, 3 ch, turn.
Row 15 1 tr in same place as turning ch, tr to last st, 3 tr in last st, 3 ch, turn.
Row 16 1 tr in each st over first front to last st, 3 tr in last st, 2 tr in first st of back, 1 tr in each st to last st of back, 2 tr in last st. (NB: Commence the back at the

point where yarn was broken off.) 3 tr in first st of first side commencing where yarn was broken off and 1 tr in each st to end. (74 sts)

Row 17 As row 2.

Rep row 17 twice.

Row 20 Dec 1st over 2, tr to last 2 sts, dec 1 st over 2. No turning ch on this row.

Row 21 1 dc, 1 htr, tr to last 3 sts, 1 htr, 1 dc, ss in last st. No turning ch.

Row 22 ss over 3 sts, 2 dc, 2 htr, tr to last 6 sts, 2 htr, 2 dc, ss in next st.

Row 23 as row 22. Break off yarn.

Join shoulder seams with dc matching 1 st of a front to 1 st at the back.

Armholes: start at underarm and work 1 dc per st at underarm, 3 dc per 2 row ends round armhole, join round with a ss.

Final row 1 ch, 1 Crab st in each st to end. Fasten off. NB: Use the Crab stitch to adjust the finish and fit of the garment.

Front/side/back edges

Starting at centre back neck join in yarn and work 1 dc to shoulder join in each st, dec 1 st over 2 round corner, work 3 dc to 2 row ends down front and 1 dc per st along base, continue like this (remembering to dec 1 st at 2nd shoulder neck point) until centre back is reached. Join with ss.

Final row Crab st to end – adjust where necessary on this row for a good fit. Fasten off.

Adding the surface crochet

1. A plain 3-branched outline using the tambour method of surface crochet was worked in scraps of deep green and shaded green mohair.
2. A large variety of brightly coloured mohair was used to make the flowers. Most of these were made in Clones knot.
3. The buds higher up the outlined stems were made with anchored clusters of varying sizes.

Fungi collage (Plate 13)

This is a slightly more elaborate method of working the nature-effects using surface crochet. A photograph was taken and the crochet worked from that.

Order of work

1) A circle of slubbed yarn was worked in double crochet to a pre-determined size. The yarn used was in fact hand-dyed but this is not essential.

2) The rotting branch was crocheted onto the circle. This was made by working 1 row dc into the fabric along the base line of the branch to give an outline on which to complete the whole. The rest of the branch was worked onto this row and initially left unattached until the required size and shape was reached. A final row of slip stitch anchored the other side of the branch to the crochet but a little toy filling was included to help give the illusion of the undulations of a rotting branch.

3) A background of 'tambour' chains was created with some of the circle quite dense. The yarn chosen was an Emu Florentine as the mixture of colours in the shade of the yarn used was, in my view, similar to the musty and mouldy appearance of rotting vegetation.

4) Next a series of knotted short length looped mohair in a variety of greens, near blues, browns, rusts, fawns, etc., created a shaggy moss effect which sprawled over the branch. This was worked in chain loops to emphasise the shagginess so that the fungi would have something to nestle into.

5) Carefully chosen chenilles and embroidery yarns were added for very small areas of other types of moss.

6) At this point the whole circle looked unalive, even uninteresting. Shadow was added at the base of the branch to give depth. An extra light off-white yarn was then introduced on the top of the small branch at the base of the circle.

7) The fungi shapes were made separately and attached with a sewing needle. As these were loose initially, it was an easy matter to find the best place for them to fit to make the completed picture.

8) A piece of hardboard was purchased to the correct diameter.

9) Holes were drilled around the edges with a sufficiently large bit to take the crochet hook.

10) As this circle of crochet was being mounted onto hardboard, it was possible to glue some padding beneath bits of the crochet, to give an increased 3-dimensional effect.

11) The final stage was to choose a complementary smooth yarn and double crochet the finished circle to the hardboard.

12) A small picture hook suitable for placing into hardboard was to hang the picture, however the drilled holes proved quite convenient and so this normal procedure was omitted.

Finally surface crochet can technically be appliquéd pieces of crochet. Any oddments of sample stitches can be added either to a garment – as in the case of the peacock cloak illustrated in *Creative Design in Crochet* where all the eyes of the peacock feathers were individually made and fringed before being sewn onto the background – *or* simply placed against a piece of driftwood for a sculpture (see figure 32).

Section F
Extensions to crochet

This final section is more an 'ideas' section than a technical one. It is hoped that the reader will be prompted to experiment for him/herself and because of this there are no actual patterns for any complete item given in this part of the book.

1. Needleweaving

This is a form of crochet that has the look of the base fabric changed by threading a tapestry needle with two or more strands of the same thickness of yarn as that that the crochet was worked in and then using the darning method of sewing to change the appearance of the crochet. The rows of crochet act as the weft (if the crochet is worked from bottom to top) and the needleweaving as the warp.

Advantages

a On a striped piece of crochet the plain and possibly stark look of the stripes can be softened and a square or tartan look result.

b If a row of colour in a multi-colour item is too vivid, drawing the eye of the onlooker to that stripe instead of the whole, needleweaving through that stripe with another colour can allow the stripe to blend in with its neighbours.

c The fabric can be made firmer with the extra process.

Disadvantages

a The strands are not anchored except at each end. This makes them susceptible to pulling, which then has to be eased back into shape.

b It can create an uneven fabric if the needleweaving is not carefully regulated. Each row has to have the same amount of yarn in it or there will be gathered parts and/or looped areas.

2. Using ribbons and braids

i) Ribbon can be threaded through the crochet fabric using either a bodkin or a small safety pin to guide it through the spaces between the crochet stitches. Long trebles are good for this kind of addition to the crochet. The asymmetrical sweater design in figure 33 has the line of the triangular neck emphasised by threading the velvet ribbon through the open cross-trebles. The one-sided 'hanky' hemline is also emphasised by the ribbon. The yarn for the background fabric was a slubbed cotton plied with a rayon knop. The triangular cap sleeves continue the theme of 'off-side' triangles. It is also worth mentioning that the stitch pattern of cross-trebles was chosen because this too gives the illusion of triangles.

(ii) Ribbons are now being manufactured with picot edges and these are ideal for inserting into fine crochet, both in fashion and as in Victorian times, into household linen.

Figure 34 shows how a crochet braid was included into a mohair sweater. Any manufacturer's ribbon or braid can be used for effects such as these.

(iii) Ribbons can be used as a yarn in themselves and the whole item can be crocheted with ribbons. Bridesmaids, headwear is one such article that is particularly suitable for crocheting in ribbon.

(iv) Braids can be appliquéd onto tailored jackets, suits, etc. There are many suitable crocheted braids to be made as well as using manufactured ones.

Advantages

a A sateen ribbon can add light reflection to a matt yarn.

b A quite different look to the texture is produced

Figure 33 *An asymmetrical hanky-style top in cotton and rayon knop*

Figure 34 *Crochet or bought braids can be incorporated into crochet design very easily*

which adds design features creating interest to an item.

c most ribbons and braids are washable and now that there is such a wide variety on the market it is possible to use a ribbon or braid that is of a complementary fibre to the basic yarn being crocheted.

Disadvantages

a Some ribbons twist if they are just loosely threaded through. If the ribbon is not double-sided as in some of the sateen ribbons, this is displeasing to the eye.

b A poor quality ribbon may not be finished along the edges and so will fray and the ragged ends then look unsightly and give the appearance of being much older than the article really is.

c Braids may not be colour-fast. Test before using. Most braids are produced for household items such as upholstery and curtain hangings, etc., and these are treated against light to prevent fading. This does not mean, however, that they are waterproof, and the dyes may run in washing.

3. Knitting with crochet

This is perhaps one of the more logical combinations as both crafts use the same basic materials.

(i) Knitting the welts and cuffs to a crochet body piece. Before the raised treble rib was popular, knitted cuffs and welts were quite common in order to maintain the elasticity throughout the life of the garment.

(ii) Panels of machine knitting can be crocheted together to produce some very beautiful items. Machine knitters are turning more and more to crochet to finish their work as the crochet hook is quick *and* effective at hems, necks and for joining.

(iii) The looseness of the knitted stitch enables the crochet hook to be inserted into the fabric very easily and so surface crochet of any description is easily added. In the recent fashion of the early 1980s, knitwear leaned strongly towards motifs. Often only one motif was necessary. In this instance a machine or stocking-stitch hand-knitted garment such as a sweater, was quickly made fashionable with a little surface crochet added to simulate the motifs popular at that time.

Tambour type surface crochet was added to the beautiful mohair jacket that was worked from a

Figure 35 *Lacy crochet pieces were made and then applied to the material to produce this beautiful nightdress and negligee set*

commercial knitting pattern (see colour plate 9). Even though the mohair gave the coat a look of exquisite luxury, a little additional mohair of equal beauty in a flame-shaded yarn lifted the whole into the exclusive range.

4. Crochet with fabrics

(i) The fine crochet laces have been added to linen and household cottons since the early 19th century and reached their peak in Queen Victoria's time in Britain. Doyleys, tablecloths, bedlinen, mantlepiece covers, antimacassars and many more household items were made from a combination of fabric and crochet 'lace'.

Apparel also had edgings of lace-style crochet added to it. In particular underwear, blouses, bonnets, and aprons.

Today the majority of people do not have the same time to spend on items that take a very long time to make and so happily it is possible to decrease that time by making open lacy crochet materials and either sewing them to fine woven fabric, or crocheting the open pattern directly onto the material.

The nightdress and negligee featured in figure 35 was made of separate pieces of crochet in a soft cotton of approximately 8's thickness, and then sewn onto the silky fabric with the sewing machine. There are two ways of doing this: one is to remove the sewing foot guide and being very careful in guiding it by hand under the machine needle, and having the fabric at the base. The other is to place a piece of tissue paper over the crochet on the sewing line, and tack it into place neatly using the same colour thread as the tackings will be machined over and it may not be possible to remove them. In this instance the crochet will not get caught in the foot and teeth guides. The nightdress and the front edge of the negligee had a narrow edging attached. This too was machined on after the crochet had been separately worked.

The little summer top (figure 36) was crocheted directly into the fabric as the material for the base of the blouse is a gloving cotton which is hardwearing and will stay in use as long as the mercerised cotton used for the yoke at the top. It had an open mesh which was very suitable indeed to accommodate the hook insertion. This meant that all the edgings and even a narrow waist tie could be crocheted without any additional preparations or processes being needed.

Further uses for crochet using the finer threads can be found for such items as handkerchiefs, bridal wear, herb sachets, etc.

(ii) Heavier materials can also be excellent fabrics to combine with crochet. During the period of fashion where shorter straight skirts were popular, the fact that there was less material in a skirt pattern made it possible for people without a lot of money to treat themselves to a length of Welsh tapestry tweed, or Scottish highland tweed.

Besides skirts, waistcoats were also very popular in the tweed fabrics. After the fashion had passed a large number of ladies were very reluctant to part with their little luxury impulse buy and so had to improvise and find other ways of using the fabric to give it an extended life. One thing about the tweeds of the hill country is their durability!

Skirts, therefore, were cut to form panels which were then used for: **a** centres of other skirt panels so that the whole could be widened and lengthened; **b** as a back and two front panels for a waistcoat or jacket; **c** as centre portions for travel luggage (holdall, shoulderbag and shopper).

Waistcoats had sleeves added and matching borders on pockets, front and neck panels, and collars.

Closely crocheted braids were added for detail particularly on the Scottish tweeds and the section on ribbons (page 105) outlines other uses.

(iii) Surface crochet into fabric is not difficult (see page 93).

5. A textile example or experiment

Often when working a sample of a craft in whatever medium, a lot of time and effort is put into it. Once the rectangle or other shape has been completed, there is a reluctance just to toss it into a drawer, never again to see the light of day. There is a limit as to the amount of wall space available in a small room, and an even greater limit to the number of peculiar gifts one can give one's friends! The batwing sweater is an idea that can be adapted to all forms of craftwork where the central panel can be the sample or experimental work in whatever craft was being tried, and the back, sleeves and side panels in a suitable weight of crochet (see figure 37).

Figure 36 *The lacy crocheted yoke was worked directly into the material as was the edging at the hem*

Method of working the panelled sweater

1) First look at the sample and decide which colour would enhance the panel. The object of putting a sampler panel into a garment is to show the sample or experiment off and not to hide its beauty, so choose a colour that will not detract from the panel itself.

2) Now determine its weight. The following may help your thinking but please remember that this section is for ideas only and that nothing in this chapter has any hard and fast rules. (In fact please remember that crochet itself has no hard and fast rules!)

   a Woven fabrics of a Welsh tapestry weight: try a pure wool Aran.

   b Woven panels with a variety of weaves: look at its flexibility and judge its weight, choose a yarn accordingly. If it is a close, even weave then the weight may determine the yarn. However, if it is a hand woven panel with irregular lines and an area of openness, try to imagine what its weight 'looks' like and choose for the look. Similarly, the beautiful open weaves should have a 2-ply or 3-ply thickness in a similar open stitch structure. No-one but yourself can make that final decision. It has to be something that will not detract from the original weaving whilst at the same time being a complementary crochet fabric that makes the whole an enjoyable exercise.

   c Embroidery panels on lightweight canvas are ideal as a panel for such a sweater. Hardanger and all drawn threadwork is equally appropriate. Here a soft fashion cotton might prove to be the correct yarn for the crochet.

   d Beading and beaded embroidery. It may be necessary to choose a double crochet fabric as the main crochet background because of the weight of the beading. It would be advisable to choose a yarn that has no elasticity, such as a cotton or linen, or a mixed fibre where some thread has been added that prevents 'give'.

   e Dyeing, such as batik: this is possible but choose carefully, it may be that the batik requires just a

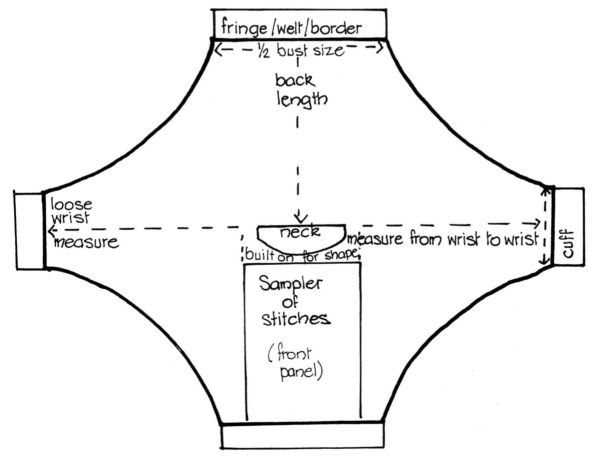

Diagram 76 Shape of paper pattern to incorporate a panel of stitches

little crochet and not as much as is being suggested in this particular pattern.

f Macrame: this is a perfect textile for such a panel. Whatever the thickness of the twine, cord, or fashion yarn used for the macrame, a similar thickness of yarn can be used for the crochet.

3) Having determined the yarn by weight and colour, draw out a paper shape as shown in diagram 76.

4) Work a tension square of the yarn that you are to use and in the stitch pattern that you have chosen. Before proceeding further, place this tension square against the panel and make quite sure in your mind that you are fully satisfied with the colour and design and that the crochet will only enhance and not detract from the panel.

5) Work the back first in whatever stitch and yarn you have chosen. It may be possible to continue down the front and sleeve in one piece. The sweater in the photograph was in fact worked in one with the only seams being those at the underarm.

6) The panel of crochet stitches was then inserted using both the yarns that had been used in the sample stitch panel of the front. Crab stitch was used in this instance.

7) Finally fringing was added at the hem using both colours beneath the central panel but only the one colour at sides and back.

6. Incorporating wood

(i) Wood can have holes drilled through it. Anything that can have holes made into it can in fact be crocheted together. The belt shown in figure 38 is just one example of small pieces of 5-ply wood being drilled to take the crochet hook. The centre of the rectangles had he the top layer of wood cut away so that the next layer showed the grain in the opposite direction. This was then burnt using a pyrography machine. Because wood, like glass and ceramics, is unbendable, it is quite important that the holes are large enough to take a hook. Similarly a hard-wearing yarn should be used to crochet the pieces together. In this instance it was jute.

(ii) The use of driftwood (see figure 32) as a base for crochet sculpture is excellent. In particular it is ideal for adding detail to nature scenes.

(iii) Besides driftwood, branches of trees, twigs, or any other natural material can be added. Colour plate 10 shows a tree sculpture which was made by a student after reading 'Lord of the Rings'.

This is a crocheted version of how I visualised 'Treebeard'. Once a project is underway, I *never* refer back to what has given me the inspiration until the whole thing is finished. Then, if it does represent the original idea, the title can be kept. However, if, during the working, other facets present themselves and changes are incorporated that alter the whole of the original idea, I still continue, just as long as what is coming off the end of the hook is pleasing and forming a composite whole.

The method of working this sculpture was to make a heavily textured trunk that would fit over a cone of plastic such as those found in cops of yarn. The plastic cones have holes in them that make them particularly useful for inserting lengths of fusewire on which to crochet the branches. Once this cone was covered, some twigs and also wire was added and crocheted over. Looped yarn was then draped over it. A student also made small buds, nodules and other 'whatever they look like we can call them that' pieces! The whole was worked and completed in less than three days at a summer school at Wolfhouse Galleries, Silverdale. The end result was just as I had visualised 'Treebeard' so when, unexpectedly and most happily, I was presented with this memento of the course, 'Treebeard' became part of the office in which I work. One of the difficulties of something like this type of crochet sculpture is that it is impossible to clean, and unless the background setting is right, it will in fact prove a misfit. Fortunately my office overlooks a canal and trees and so the sculpture fits in excellently.

7. Adding leather

Perhaps the use of suede and leather in crochet is not too uncommon these days. The leather is easily punched with a leather punch at whatever size hole that is needed for the yarn and for the crochet hook being used. The waistcoat of rectangular suede pieces (figure 14) has already been described. Almost any of the patchwork templates that are used by the patchwork embroiderers and quilters should be practical for cutting out leather/suede shapes. One point to remember here is that if a diamond or triangle is being used it will be necessary to round off the acute corners to avoid them poking through the crochet stitches.

Irregular shapes of sheepskin or attractively marked

Figure 37 *The central panel was a piece of crochet with no two rows of crochet in the lighter yarn being the same. This panel could be substituted by any form of experimental craft/textile sample and the yarn changed to suit accordingly*

Figure 38 *Pieces of wood crocheted together to form a belt*

leather can be incorporated into crochet in exactly the same way as the irregular crochet motif (page 58) is incorporated into other crochet. Many interesting garments and accessories can be made in this way.

The waistcoat of Rita Williams in blue suede, was cut from a large piece of suede with the idea of incorporating chevron stripes of yarn. Rita made the waistcoat at a summer school on a five-day course and came armed with the suede and yarn and a determination to have exactly what she could see in her mind's eye. The result was well worth the effort although it took some time for her to fully understand the principle of making chevrons, which was essential before the suede could be cut to shape to fit the tension piece of crochet. Usually when working with suede, leather, or sheepskin, the crochet complements the leather. In this instance the leather had to fit the crochet stripe!

Finally leather and suede can be appliquéd on as can any crochet motif. The Lancaster skyline collage is an example of appliquéd leather, although the base edge and some of the castle turrets did have holes punched through to accommodate the yarn and neaten the edges. (See colour plate 11). The background crochet for the sunset was eventually selected after many experiments. Not for a long time was Tunisian crochet thought of as a possible solution but after repeated failures with the sky more prominent than the skyline as the stitches stood out and overpowered the leather, a 'happy accident' prompted me to think that the Tunisian simple stitch could be the solution. As can be seen, this was in fact the final choice.

8. Wire

Fusewire can be bent very easily and so can copper and silver wires. Crochet in this medium is attractive and quite practical for some items. The colour plate 12 shows a hat, cuffs and deep necklace crocheted in fuse wire for a dramatic effect. The stage lights are picked up and reflected in the wire, which should not tarnish if treated wire is used. As mentioned in the section on wood, wire can also be used to crochet over for firmness in all forms of sculptures.

9. Mixtures

Any mixture of any crafts can be blended with a little care and forethought. Similarly any mixture of the various aspects of crochet can be blended. The pink shrug featured on the front cover is an example of this, being an 'unfinished symphony'. Every time the jacket is to be modelled, something else gets added. The making of this garment went through the following stages:

1) Basic Tunisian square of simple stitch but with much colour blending using different shades of the same hue. (This was the experiment that eventually got the Lancaster Skyline correct.)
2) Border of shell stitches of different lengths.
3) Broomstick sleeves with a lacy crochet pattern between.
4) Surface crochet over some of the frills on the border to make them more solid.
5) The back design was crocheted in tambour crochet/embroidery and sequins and other 'bits' were applied.
6) A final edging.

At this stage the jacket was worn.

Subsequently: further sequins were added to the back and shoulder details; ribbons were threaded through the sleeves; an extra 'fill-in' row was added to the border; a front fastener was created.

Other ideas present themselves at each wearing *but* like all good things there has to be a time to stop as the next addition will prove to be the 'over-kill' and the design is then no longer a good one.

10. Conclusion

Endless possibilities still remain uncovered. To me, as to so many, the versatility, flexibility and ability of crochet to complement other media is a constant source of delight.

As I remarked before, crochet has not yet been mechanised and will not be mechanised in the forseeable future, so crochet is automatically 'hand made' – a prize in itself.

No yarn is: too thin to be worked; too thick; too smooth; or too textured.

The fibre content also need hold no fears as long as the style of design and stitch pattern has been chosen with the fibre/yarn in mind and not a design made for which a yarn has to be found. Let the yarn 'talk' to you and suggest the stitch pattern or shape.

The secret of originality in crochet design is to have an open mind, to be experimental, and to ensure the design is for the person and place it is to enhance and *not* based on one's own preferences. Obviously the designer/crochet worker has to feel comfortable with the work whilst in progress, and know it is going to be exactly right in the end or the final article will be stilted or 'over-dressed' or, alternatively, carelessly completed.

It only remains for me to tell you to enjoy your crocheting, and not to be afraid to experiment.

Crochet terms & international signs

UK		USA		International Signs
ch	chain			⬭ or •
ss	slip stitch	slst		⌒ or ⬤
dc	double crochet	sc	single crochet	✕
Crst	Crab stitch			
tr	treble	dc	double crochet	⊤
Rtr	raised treble	Rdc	raised double crochet	
RtrF	raised treble front	RdcF	raised double crochet forward	⌐⊥
RtrB	raised treble back	RdcB	raised double crochet backward	⊥⌐
3trcl	three treble cluster	3dccl	three double crochet cluster	⋀ or ⊕
dtr	double treble	tr	treble	⧦
tr tr	triple treble	dtr	double treble	⧻
quad tr	quad treble	tr tr	triple treble	⧻
htr	half treble	hdc	half double crochet	⊤

General abbreviations

st	stitch
cl	cluster
lp	loop
patt	pattern
yoh	yarn over hook
inc	increase
dec	decrease
tog	together
bet	between
gr	group
sp	space
rnd	round
RS	right side
WS	wrong side
RH	right hand
LH	left hand
M	main colour
C1	first contrast
C2	second contrast
DK	doubleknit thickness

Hook sizes

International Standard Range (ISR)	United Kingdom Wool (old nos.)	Cotton (old nos.)	United States Wool		Cotton
10.00 mm					
9.00 mm	000		15		
	00		13		
8.00 mm	0		12		
	1		11		
7.00 mm	2		10½	K	
	3		10	J	
6.00 mm	4		9	I	
5.50 mm	5		8	H	
5.00 mm	6		7		
4.50 mm	7		6	G	
4.00 mm	8		5	F	
3.50 mm	9		4	E	
			3	D	
3.00 mm	10	3/0	2	C	
	11	2/0			0
2.50 mm	12	0	1	B	1
	13	1	0		2
					3
2.00 mm	14	1½			4
		2			5
1.75 mm		2½			6
		3			
1.50 mm		3½			7
		4			8
1.25 mm		4½			9
		5			10
1.00 mm		5½			11
		6			12
0.75 mm		6½			13
0.60 mm		7			14
		7½			
		8			

Supplies

All yarns are available at good department stores and wool shops throughout the country. Should you have any difficulty in obtaining materials contact the Crochet Design Centre, White Cross, South Road, Lancaster LA1 4XH.

Index